*Choosing Books for Children*

# Choosing Books for Children

## *A Commonsense Guide*

## BETSY HEARNE

DELACORTE PRESS/NEW YORK

*For my mother,*
*who gave life long after she gave birth*

Published by
Delacorte Press
1 Dag Hammarskjold Plaza
New York, N.Y. 10017

Manufactured in the United States of America
9 8 7 6 5 4 3 2

LIBRARY OF CONGRESS CATALOGING IN PUBLICATION DATA

Hearne, Betsy Gould.
Choosing books for children.

Includes bibliographies.
1. Children—Books and reading.  2. Children's
literature.  I. Title.
Z1037.A1H42     028.5′5     80-66203
ISBN 0-385-28210-9
(previously ISBN 0-440-01930-3)

Acknowledgments on the following pages will serve
as an extension of the copyright page.

## ACKNOWLEDGMENTS

"Amelia Mixed the Mustard" by A. E. Housman: Used by permission of The Society of Authors as the literary representative of the Estate of A. E. Housman.

"Hannah Bantry in the Pantry" and Illustration: From A GREAT BIG UGLY MAN CAME UP AND TIED HIS HORSE TO ME by Wallace Tripp. Text and illustrations copyright © 1973 by Wallace Tripp. By permission of Little, Brown and Company.

Excerpt from NATURAL HISTORY by M. B. Goffstein: Copyright © 1979 by M. B. Goffstein. Reprinted by permission of Farrar, Straus & Giroux, Inc.

Excerpt from THE BOY WHO WAS FOLLOWED HOME by Margaret Mahy: Copyright © 1975. Used by permission of Franklin Watts, Inc.

Excerpt from THE TWO OF THEM by Aliki: Used by permission of William Morrow & Company, Inc.

"Rabbits Have Fur . . ." by Ray Fabrizzio: From MAGIC LIGHTS AND STREETS OF SHINING JET edited by Dennis Saunders. Copyright © 1978 by Dennis Saunders. Published by William Morrow & Company, Inc. Every effort has been made to locate the proprietor of this material. If the proprietor will write to the publisher, formal arrangements will be made.

Title page illustration, "Where the Sidewalk Ends," and text of "Early Bird" and "Recipe for a Hippopotamus Sandwich" from WHERE THE SIDEWALK ENDS: The Poems and Drawings of Shel Silverstein. Copyright © 1974 by Shel Silverstein. By permission of Harper & Row, Publishers, Inc.

"Toads" by Valerie Worth: From MORE SMALL POEMS by Valerie Worth. Copyright © 1976 by Valerie Worth. Reprinted by permission of Farrar, Straus & Giroux, Inc.

## A Note from the Author

I would like to acknowledge The American Library
Association for granting me a leave to write this book,
and to thank my staff, especially Barbara Elleman and
Denise Wilms, whose intelligent and unresting efforts
made it possible for me to take time away from a review journal that has come out every two weeks—
rain, shine, blizzard, drought, tornado, death, de-
pression, strike, inflation, or disaster—since 1905. May
*Booklist* continue to flourish. Marilyn Kaye also gets
a round of applause for annotating the booklists.

The lists of books at the end of each chapter represent some of my own favorites. I purposely limited
them to only a few because long bibliographies seem
overwhelming. These lists offer a good starting point
for anyone interested in exploring books for children,
but, like any selection of books, my guide is personal
and should be altered by readers to fit their own
tastes. The examples mentioned in the text by title
and author are also prime choices and are available
in most libraries and bookstores. Tracking down
these titles will further enrich the variety of books
not mentioned here only because of limited space.

# Contents

ix

# CONTENTS

## *Trying to Be Human*

# 1

When I first discovered children's books, I was well on my way to becoming a musician and needed money. Never did hunger lead to such a feast. It's now my profession to read and evaluate nearly all of the books published for children each year.

The magic of books, children, and books and children brought together hooked me. It was not an interest in education or a case of arrested development or even a child of my own. Those are all inspiring motivations, but for me it was seeing a river at its source, the spring of the imagination. This was not dainty tiptoe magic, but a cauldron of stories.

Children's books are not only charming but charmed, in the most powerful sense. The child is the beginning of life; the story is the beginning of literature. People and stories are deeply connected. It took many years for me to discover the full possibilities of children's books for family growth or for any relationship between adults and children. Storytelling, reading, and child caring flow together in a natural way. Children's books offer every family a humane balance for time-clock living, a chance to pause and take a fresh look at each other.

Think, for example, of the classic five o'clock conversation:

"How was school today?"

"OK . . ." (child kicking table)

"Don't kick the table, dear. . . . What did you do?"

"Oh, nothing."

Can you hear the long awkward pauses and communication breakdown? There is another possibility.

"How're you doing?"

"OK . . ."

"I like that weird poster you put up in your room yesterday."

"It's not weird."

"Well, wild. Stop kicking the table, dear. Anyway, it reminded me of how much I used to love science fiction movies. In fact, I bought a terrific book today —science fiction. Want to look at it tonight?"

"OK . . . where is it?"

Few children will turn down an invitation to do something with an enthusiastic parent.

The first conversation is a dead end, but the second one crosses a bridge toward a shared world. The child can be teething on the table or drinking a first cup of coffee. Books can bridge any age and interest.

A parent preoccupied by work can take a break reading *The Story of Ferdinand* to a child at bedtime. An aunt, uncle, or friend can spark or rekindle acquaintance just by sitting with a child on the couch and reading a chapter of C. S. Lewis's *The Lion, the Witch, and the Wardrobe.* Grandparents can share *The Lord of the Rings* with a high school student. There's no better way of relating to the young than over a bridge of books.

This book tells how, what, when, and where. You may want to skip around or you may want to see how the literature grows with the child. There's a chapter for every age group. There's a book for every situation. There's a world waiting for you and the children you love.

## *For All Ages—Just Born or Reborn*

# 2

It's amazing that children's learning to read is considered important but children's *books* are not. Plastic toys sell. Books don't. If children's minds are important, so are their books.

There is a literature good enough to match any child's freshness, interest, and honesty. Mother Goose is still one of the best sources of nursery rhymes, but her offspring have flown the coop and multiplied into thousands of picture books, novels, and nonfiction. Unfortunately, there are many readers, both child and adult, who haven't had the chance to know or enjoy them.

The gap between books and readers comes from a basic problem in our society. Children are loved in their place, but their place is too far from what "really counts"—money, power, and prestige. Their books, too, are held at arm's length from the literature that "really counts"—adult literature. This isn't because of quality—adult best sellers rarely approach Shakespeare —but because in most cases children aren't considered a real part of adult work and play. It's easy for children and adults to become strangers to each other's minds.

Books loved and shared can build a bridge where the standard question-and-answer conversations fail. Is there any real reply to "My, how you've grown!"? Try it at a cocktail party; it's a real conversation stopper. Most adults talk to children as if they were a breed apart. They may even feel at a loss in talking with children at all.

Even a parent can have this problem. Parents trust the education of their children to a school. If their heirs can't read, they logically blame the school system. Too few parents know how to get involved in reading with their kids. If they try, it often turns out to be either a chore (boring book) or a concession (cute book), but most often it is not a pleasure. They've picked a book at random because they don't know where to start.

Librarians have been pioneers in channeling children's books into mainstream literature, for both critical examination and popular consumption. But the library's role as patron of art and literature for children is endangered. Tax cuts and the decline in school-age population have booted children's books back down to the bottom of social concerns.

Literature is vital to children's reading and learning. But the survival of children's books is crucial to more than children. Children's books are a matter of adult self-interest as well. There is a child in every adult and an adult in every child and it is a tragic thing to see them separated. They can both get a lot out of children's books, just as their ancestors did out of myths, folktales, and fairy stories. The power of story is not to be denied. In prehistoric caves, during Irish famines, in Nazi concentration camps, stories were as important as food. They were sometimes served instead, and they nourished starving hearts.

Children's literature is the inheritance of this tradition. It can be as good or as bad as adult literature. The good is inspired and inspiring. The mediocre is unmemorably entertaining. The bad may be cute and dull instead of obscene and dull. There are best sellers, literary award winners, unrecognized works of lasting merit, classics, and escape reading.

Today's children are tomorrow's reading adults. If today's adults don't care about children's imaginations or their books, if they don't sense the strong connection, children certainly won't. Today's adults will lose a golden opportunity for pleasure, and tomorrow's adults may lose the passion for literature and learning.

Children deserve the best you give people you care for. It doesn't take an educational study to show that children do what you do, not what you tell them to do. And it doesn't take a market survey to show that you do what you *like* to do, not what you ought to do. If you like to read to yourself and your children, they will like reading to themselves and their children.

What really hooks anyone on children's books is

liking them—not their importance, but their artistry and appeal. Children's literature is born of an art that has roots in storytelling older than telling time. It casts a spell that will work by itself if given the chance. The reading relationship between you and your children can shape their feelings and reshape your own.

Childhood is the time and children's books are the place for powerful emotions, powerful language, powerful art. If the book you're reading seems boring, toss it. The book probably *is* boring, and there are thousands that aren't. The trick is to find one that casts a spell over you both. There is no room for cutesy books, dull books, or books that talk down. Children are not inferior. They are small but they feel, think, listen, and see just as much as adults. Some feel, think, listen, and see more.

Whatever the sensitivity ratio, there are books that can hold both child and adult. During the last several decades there has been a quiet revolution in children's literature, but most people don't know about it. There are approximately 2,500 new juvenile trade books (not textbooks) published each year. There are some 40,000 books in print—which range from bad to glorious.

Feeding your child strained banana, hamburgers, or eventually filet mignon can't beat sharing books like *Where the Wild Things Are* or *Watership Down*. Feeding minds, your own and your children's, is tantalizing. The best menu includes the kind of book that nourishes you both. Obligation will get you nowhere —it's pleasure that counts. The bedtime story that does not bore a parent leads to a book discussion that does not bore an adolescent. Books do not make you fat, do not lead to drunken disorder, and do not cause cancer. That in itself makes them a rare treat.

The best children's writers say things to a five-year-old that a fifty-year-old can also respect. The two may not see the *same* thing, but each will see *some*thing. Speaking to differing age levels requires a skillful simplicity in dealing with complex issues, actions, and emotions. A large concept can be boiled down to pithy but no less punchy language that means something to all ages.

The ability to say so much with simple language has characterized the best of children's literature from its beginning, but lately there have been some startling advances. As an art form, children's books have been raised to a new level by some of the best writers and artists in America and Britain, my emphasis being on books written in English. Before the age of one, a baby can see a song or verse translated into art propped up on a lap in the form of a book. Some of the most beautiful books available are illustrated lullabies, songs, and nursery rhymes (there's a list at the end of Chapter 3).

Why bother with beautiful? Beautiful is expensive, and this baby can hardly focus its eyes yet—or maybe the creature's advanced to drawing on the table with a banana. The answer is two-fold, the first being yourself. Looking at dull, cartoon-type pictures is a form of persecution. Reading trite jingles doubles the agony . . . which leads to the second reason. Why foist bad stuff off on the smallest members of the community?

Children are a product of their environment. Their mentality will grow with what they hear and see. The price of a book isn't really too much to pay for developing an instinct for quality.

The songs a mother, father, and grandparent sing to a baby, the nursery rhymes they chant, are deeply imbedded literature. When I was nursing my daughter, Bob Dylan happened to be one of my favorite songwriters. I had named the baby Joanna, in fact, after Dylan's song "Visions of Johanna." The song I sang her most often was "Just Like Tom Thumb's Blues," which is a musically soothing but lyrically morbid number that fits in well to the rocking chair motion. Through long, tired nights of infant colic and crying, I can remember singing. I don't know whether I sang for me or for her, but it always put both of us to sleep. Long after I had stopped nursing and stopped rocking and even stopped singing lullabies, I happened to hum "Just Like Tom Thumb's Blues," and the same baby who was now six stood entranced in the middle of the kitchen and begged to hear the song again.

The point is that whatever you do counts. It all enters into the child's consciousness at a deep unconscious level. You can quote Shakespeare, sing Dylan, push Disney, or read a children's book. The sights and sounds surrounding a very young child, even a newborn, may not be understood, but they will be impressed. Whatever children hear and whatever they look at is important.

There is vital literature from infant to young adult, but infancy is a logical starting point for everything, including literature. And what comes first? There is nothing more satisfying than putting something in the mouth. What goes into the mouth goes into the mind. Let it be literature as well as plastic. Songs and sucking; cardboard, cloth, and chewing; paper, pictures, and pointing; language and listening—it's such a natural progression of events. While you and the baby are regularly enjoying lap-sitting sessions of singing a book or saying nursery rhymes and enjoying their illustrations, the baby will, some bright and unexpected day, try to grab the book and eat it.

Well, why not? How often have you chewed on a thought? Give a child the same chance. There is nothing wrong with familiarity, with the book as a physical companion. The things dearest to us always get the most wear, whether they are teddy bears or blue jeans. I have seen children hug books they love. For crawlers and toddlers, "physical" and "mental" are one and the same game—the exploration of an unknown world through taste, sound, touch, sight, smell. *Every* book is a scratch-and-sniff book for children, or more likely a scratch-sniff-and-chew book. They are getting comfortable with the book as part of living. Soon they'll be ready to yell "DOG" when they see one in the book. Language is a magical bridge from physical to conceptual. Finally they'll be ready to hear that word magically transformed into a dog story with a beginning, middle, and end. "Once upon a time there was a dog, and . . ."

Story is suspense, and the power of a story runs almost as deep as the power of song or rhythmic rhyme. Two-year-olds are ready for stories, in pictures and in words. They are ready for the first great segment of children's literature, the picture book. The picture book will lead to longer stories, the stories to novels and nonfiction. As for you the adult—you are just in time. The story is about to begin.

## *The Bookstore Blues—Browsing for Somebody Younger*

# 3

It's easy for a birthday to sneak up on you. Suddenly one of your favorite children is celebrating again— cake, ice cream, and presents. Here's the golden opportunity: a good book will (1) last a long time and (2) be enjoyed over and over again. March right out and invest in the future.

So there you are in a bookstore, surrounded with books, *lost* among books. Perhaps they seem expensive. You can justify the expense: quality costs. Paperbacks are inexpensive and high quality. Libraries are free. The question is, how do you tell a good children's book from a bad one?

I used to buy a copy of *Winnie the Pooh* every time I got a birth announcement. There's nothing wrong with *Winnie the Pooh*, but sometimes I wanted a little *variation*, especially if I was going to be the visitor who read bedtime stories in a couple of years. Later, as a parent who was going to read bedtime stories every night, I wanted *more* than a little variation.

The same old question haunts the aisles of every children's book department: What's a good book for young Herbert going on *x* years old? Salespeople can't always lay the question to rest. They sometimes don't know where to start any more than the buyer. They don't know the child and may not even be familiar with children's books. Buyer and seller are stuck in the myth that children and their books are a breed apart from adult tastes and interests.

Take heart, because it's not so difficult to make the connection. Rule number one: don't panic and grab a copy of *Black Beauty* because your grandmother recommended it to you in your youth. Stand there and calmly ask yourself how you pick out a good coat. Color? Cut? Fabric? Warmth? Is it going to wear well? Do you just like the way it looks? Picking a good children's book is as easy as making any purchase. Actually, it's more like deciding why you like a movie. Was it the story, the characters, the scenery?

When you pick up a picture book and read it, first ask yourself an important and helpful question. Is it clever or boring? Look at the illustrations slowly, carefully. That's the way a child will do it. Can you live with them? Do they entertain you or do they look like "kid stuff," pictures anyone could do with their toes? You are the key here, because if you enjoy the book, your children will soak it up. They won't get half as much pleasure stuck off alone with something you don't like well enough to share in, and you really won't want to be left out of the fun either. Trust your feelings.

The same kind of personal involvement in both book and child pays off long past the picture-book stage. If you're looking for something informational, pick a topic that interests you as well as the child. Ask for a book on bugs or ballet and then read some of it. It should seem clear, accurate, and interesting *to you*. If you're searching for stories or novels for older children, read a bit there, too, just the way you'd browse through a book rack at the airport. Something will catch your attention. Tastes and interests vary as much in children's books as they do in adult books. They're also contagious from adult to child. Parents especially pass their tastes and interests on to their children, whether it's football, rock collecting, or plumbing repair.

The same goes for books. Reading can be the same kind of shared activity as fishing, playing cards, or going to a ball game or concert. Your own individual reaction to a children's book, linked to your own involvement with the child, is as important as any expert's recommendation.

There always seems to be the insolvable question of what age can understand and enjoy what book, but that is not as big a mystery as it may seem. You can sense when a child is ready to try solid food, play alone outside, start piano lessons, or take the car for a date.

It's all a blend of skills and knowledge, interest and experience.

The size of a child's mind is more flexible than sleeve length, especially when an adult plans to join in the operation and share the book. But there are some ball-park estimates:

> For ages two to six, picture books have illustrations on every page and very little text. Picture books are meant to be read aloud and the pictures pored over.

> For ages seven to nine, beginning-to-read books will have short episodic chapters, scattered illustrations, and simple vocabulary, slightly enlarged type, an open, friendly format, and a plot and cast of characters without too many complications. They can be read aloud to youngsters or alone by the child as reading skills start to develop.

> For ages ten to thirteen there is a wide range of fiction, depending on a child's interest, motivation, and reading ease. This "middle-grade" audience has a variety to choose from—comedy, tragedy, mystery, romance, adventure, fantasy, and realism. The format looks like a short novel.

Nonfiction, poetry, and folklore cover the gamut of interests for all ages from preschool to high school. If you know someone's hobbies or interests, you probably know their abilities, especially if you take the opportunity to talk books or read together. Your own involvement is the key. Sometimes having the child along helps, for the outing can turn into a party.

Evaluating children's books is a matter of practice as well as taste. The best way to start is with a few touchstone titles, surefire suggestions that rarely miss. Once you've experienced something really good, it will be hard to grab any old thing off the shelf. Having the background on what's happened since *Black Beauty* may help.

The social and political upsets of the 1960s were reflected in children's books as well as protest movements. Maurice Sendak's *Where the Wild Things Are* was a turning-point title for young children, Louise Fitzhugh's *Harriet the Spy* for middle-grade readers, and S. E. Hinton's *The Outsiders* for junior high and high school kids. These three represented a trend of tackling children's emotional reality head-on with high standards of art and writing. When these books were published they were mightily protested by the educational establishment because they touched some "negative" aspects of childhood or society that adults didn't particularly want to deal with out in the open in front of their children. Their children, of course, were already dealing with them.

In *Where the Wild Things Are*, a little boy named Max gets mad after his mother punishes him for misbehaving. He dreams of running wild with monsters, as their lord and master, empowered by the trick of "staring into all their yellow eyes." What seemed to alarm people about the book was the terror those monsters might strike into the heart of any child who beheld them. The book does, in fact, deal with basic

emotions. Children have always sensed that neither
Max's anger nor his monsters ever get out of control,
and they love his freewheeling fantasy, based as it is
in such a secure framework. Not only does Max tame
the monsters, but when he wakes up his mother has
brought him supper, and it's still hot!

Fitzhugh's novel *Harriet the Spy* faced an even
more serious charge than frightening children. Many
adults were afraid it would motivate them to mis-
behave! Harriet was not a traditional innocent heroine, nor were her parents the traditionally wise and
attentive sort. Some educators were sure that juvenile
spy clubs would spring up all over the country under
Harriet's influence. As it turned out, children simply
recognized Harriet as one of themselves, imperfect
but surviving the odds of growing up in the best way
she could. Kids loved her.

A similar fear of rebellion inspired protest against
the teenage novel *The Outsiders*, by S. E. Hinton,
which dealt with gang warfare, death, and adolescent
alienation. Hinton's characters were faced with harsh
reality. The gauntlet had been thrown. Children's
literature had moved into a new age.

All three books became wildly popular and have
achieved the status of classics. They now appear mild
in contrast to later developments. These three titles
certainly serve to update the newcomer whose hand
wavers uncertainly toward *Black Beauty*.

Earlier classic choices such as *The Hobbit*, *Charlotte's Web*, and *Little House on the Prairie* don't
need much advertisement. They've already been "discovered" by adults. These well-known titles are a good

starting point, but in fact there are children's books as appealing as *Charlotte's Web* that aren't yet household words.

Regrettably, children's literature suffers from tokenism. There are two famous annual children's book awards, the Newbery Medal for writing and the Caldecott Medal for illustration, but the annual winners of these awards are simply two of scores of good books published each year. The handful of children's best sellers, including the picture books of Richard Scarry and Dr. Seuss and the novels of Judy Blume, don't begin to represent the wide range of books available.

For example, take the work of picture-book illustrator William Steig. Steig is a cartoonist for *The New Yorker* magazine, and a lot of people know his drawings, if not his name. Not nearly so many recognize his work for children, which is outstanding. *The Amazing Bone* is my favorite. In it, Pearl, a lovely young pig, is appreciating the first day of spring when she has the good fortune to run into a talking bone and, shortly thereafter, the misfortune of meeting a hungry fox. Perhaps there are only four plots in the world, and this one certainly isn't unusual. But there is a rainbow of variations, and this is one of the brightest.

Just as Beatrix Potter does in *Peter Rabbit,* Steig uses the choicest words without worrying whether children can understand them or not. For children do understand much more than we give them credit for, especially in the context of a story. "It was a brilliant day, and instead of going straight home from school, Pearl dawdled." What a wonderful word, "dawdled."

What an appropriate word for children. We are treated to a picture of a succulent young porker dressed in romantic pink and dreaming of exciting things to come.

It's the little details that count. Pearl expects to be eaten soon. Readers know this is not going to happen, if for no other reason than the irrepressibly cheerful colors, but the suspense is heightened by Steig's straight-faced wit. " 'I hope it won't all take too long,' said Pearl. She could smell vinegar and oil. The fox was preparing a salad to go with his meal." What brings about her escape is a suddenly remembered incantation from the bone. When parent and child say that incantation together, villains shrink away.

Picture books for young children make up a whole world to explore. Steig's work serves as an example to set standards for comparing the many offerings on the shelf for toddlers and primary school children.

As to touchstone titles for older children, Natalie Babbitt deserves a place in every heart for crafting the novel *Tuck Everlasting*. In this book, an eleven-year-old girl discovers a secret stream that makes anyone who drinks from it live forever. Babbitt's words are chosen with care and humor. The first sentence of Tuck is a perfect example: "The road that led to Treegap had been trod out long before by a herd of cows who were, to say the least, relaxed." Anyone who knows cows can spot them in that sentence, and anyone who doesn't know cows can find out about them right there in that word "relaxed." In fact, the whole first paragraph of the Prologue makes a reader see sharply and clearly:

The first week of August lands at the very top of summer, the top of the live-long year, like the highest seat of a Ferris wheel when it pauses in its turning. The weeks that come before are only a climb from balmy spring, and those that follow a drop to the chill of autumn, but the first week in August is motionless, and hot. It is curiously silent, too, with blank white dawns and glaring noons, and sunsets smeared with too much color. Often at night there is lightning, but it quivers all alone. There is no thunder, no relieving rain. These are strange and breathless days, the dog days, when people are led to do things they are sure to be sorry for after.

The plot of *Tuck Everlasting* is tightly wound and the setting is hauntingly real. This book is for a more advanced reader, but simple books can be just as good. Simple does not mean simplistic; witness some of the wonderful writing that has found its way into beginning readers. If there is an underlying principle behind children's literature, it's the kind of simplicity that does not lessen the book but adds a new glint to it. And that goes for poetry, non-fiction, and illustration as well as stories.

Not that children's books can't be complicated. British poet Ted Hughes, for instance, collaborated with artist Leonard Baskin to produce a sophisticated book of poetry called *Season Songs*, a remarkable book that sings when read aloud. The quality of poetry, however, does not depend on complexity of language. Simple, more accessible work can be equally skillful.

Take, for example, A. E. Housman's little narrative poem, "Amelia Mixed the Mustard":

> *Amelia mixed the mustard.*
> *She mixed it good and thick;*
> *She put it in the custard*
> *And made her mother sick,*
> *And showing satisfaction*
> *By many a loud huzza*
> *"Observe," said she, "the action*
> *Of mustard on Mama."*

What could be more vivid than this character who steps onstage and just as quickly steps right off again?

In nonfiction, Milton Meltzer has written one of the most extensive thoughtful studies ever published, for children. *Never to Forget: The Jews of the Holocaust* is a well-organized history supported by first-person accounts of survivors and by the recovered documents of slain victims. This book, however, is for older readers in junior or senior high school.

The same kind of accuracy and interest has been captured in pictorial nonfiction by David Macaulay's architectural history series: *Cathedral, City, Pyramid, Underground,* and *Castle.* Each combines sweeping black-and-white drawings and diagrams with carefully researched and selected facts. Macaulay's books attract fourth graders, college students, and anyone with a sense of curiosity because they're *well done and accessible.* That combination seems to be the key characteristic of books that please adults as well as children, and it's a high standard to live up to.

Macaulay's books are just plain interesting to everybody. You won't find a better introduction to his subjects anywhere.

On the very simplest level, Joanna Cole and Jerome Wexler do the same thing in their scientific presentation for preschoolers and primary school children, *A Chick Hatches*. Step by step, with photographs that are almost translucent and terms that are exact but always clear, the writer and the photographer together show an everyday event for the miracle it really is.

High standards at an accessible level exist for illustration as well. Nancy Burkert is a highly respected artist. Her paintings for *Snow White and the Seven Dwarfs* (translated by Randall Jarrell) raise illustration to a fine art. The pictures demand the reader's attention. They are placed alternately with the text so that you have to read aloud and listen to the words, then take the time to absorb what the paintings portray as well. It is an experience worth the pause. This is the kind of book an adult doesn't rush through for the child's sake, wanting to get it over with in a hurry. It's the kind of book an adult and child love together.

On the other hand, an especially wiggly five-year-old might not be able to wade through such long stretches of reading without being able to look at something. It takes practice to work up an attention span, though it's worth learning and it's something many children can't manage these days. The active types might enjoy Trina Schart Hyman's paintings for *Snow White*. There are pictures to look at with every page of print and they move at a more dramatic pace. It's fascinating to see children respond to utterly

different approaches to the same story. The possibilities for enjoying fairy tales and folktales are endless.
Nursery rhymes are just as rich. Those verses sometimes make more sense than nonsense. It's worth looking at the multitude of Mother Goose books available
before picking one out. Some of them are guaranteed
to make you smile as surely as they do the child. The
offhand hues, squiggly lines, and comic-satiric view of
Wallace Tripp in *A Great Big Ugly Man Came Up
and Tied His Horse to Me: A Book of Nonsense Verse*
is story art at its funniest. There is one picture of an
elite dinner party to go with this rhyme:

> *Hannah Bantry, in the pantry,*
> *Gnawing at a mutton bone;*
> *How she gnawed it,*
> *How she clawed it,*
> *When she found herself alone.*

While Hannah cowers, chewing greedily, the guests
sit under a picture of several lions crossing in front
of a stream. The picture is labeled "Pride Goeth
Before a Fall"—far from the main focus of the illustration, but a side joke for the sharp-eyed. Tripp's
characters are often political cartoons, as were most of
the original Mother Goose rhymes.

A well-stocked bookstore will have many such touchstone titles to browse through. A good library can
offer hours of browsing for you and the child together.
A book you really love may persuade you to start your
own permanent collection. The bookstore and the

library can use your full support, just as you can use their full resources. They offer the same kind of service that a fine restaurant does—for less money—in offering both a choice assortment and ideas for home cooking. The answer to that question of how to tell a good children's book from a bad one is the same as telling a good recipe from a bad one. You just taste it.

Looking and reading are the test. With a little time and interest, anyone can be a first-class, four-star, triple-A children's book connoisseur, and glad of the experience.

## CHAPTER 3

### *An Example for Every Age*

FITZHUGH, LOUISE. *Harriet the Spy* (8–12). Harper & Row (hardcover); Dell Yearling (paper).
The zany adventures of 11-year-old Harriet, who learns more than she expects by keeping a secret notebook about family and friends.

GRAHAME, KENNETH. *The Wind in the Willows* (8 & up). Scribner's (hardcover); Dell Yearling (paper).
A romantic water rat, a peaceful mole, and a majestic badger conspire to keep their boastful friend Toad out of trouble in this cozy, exuberant story of life in the Wild Wood.

MACAULAY, DAVID. *Castle* (6 & up). Houghton Mifflin.

Finely detailed illustrations explore the construction of an imaginary castle in all its grandeur and glory.

POTTER, BEATRIX. *Peter Rabbit* (3–6). Warne (hardcover); (several paperback editions available).

Charming illustrations capture the humor and excitement in this beloved tale of a mischievous rabbit who narrowly escapes disaster.

SENDAK, MAURICE. *Where the Wild Things Are* (5–8). Harper & Row.

Naughty Max runs away to revel in the land of the wild things, but soon finds he'd rather be back home, where someone loves him best of all.

STEIG, WILLIAM. *The Amazing Bone* (5–8). Farrar, Straus & Giroux (hardcover); Puffin (paper).

A succulent pig and her loyal bone foil the intentions of a wily fox.

TOLKIEN, J. R. R. *The Hobbit* (8 & up). Houghton Mifflin (hardcover); Ballantine (paper).

Elves, trolls, and goblins engage in battles and quests in this compelling, enduring fantasy saga.

TRIPP, WALLACE. *A Great Big Ugly Man Came Up and Tied His Horse to Me* (5–8). Little, Brown (hardcover and paper).

The jolliest of pictures depict the silliest of situations in this collection of nonsense verse.

WHITE, E. B. *Charlotte's Web* (5–8). Harper & Row (hardcover and paper).

Wilbur the Pig realizes true friendship and loyalty when a remarkably talented spider saves his life.

WILDER, LAURA INGALLS. *Little House on the Prairie* (8–12). Harper & Row (hardcover and paper). Laura's story of her family's move to the Kansas frontier captures the adventures and drama of everyday pioneer life.

## The Picture Book for
## Younger Children—Dead or Alive?

# 4

Analyzing picture books reminds me of a time in freshman biology lab when I was handed a frog and told to dissect it for an anatomy exam. As faithfully as I had studied the diagram—stomach here, brain there, tubes and muscles everywhere—I could not seem to lay out that frog and locate the parts that existed so clearly and neatly in the labeled diagram. I even sneaked it into my pocket and out of the lab for further study in the girls' bathroom, which, on account of my roommate's protest, was the only spot available in the dormitory for such activity. What I discovered, besides a lot of now-forgotten biology terms and the panic that can strike coeds stumbling over frog parts which are strewn across a dimly lit

bathroom at midnight, was this: *every frog is different.*
Theory and life don't always fit together.

There is no such thing as a theoretical book. You
can talk about what makes a good children's book—
or any good book—till you're blue in the face, but
the real live book is a one-of-a-kind experience. Which
leads me to another major principle I discovered on
that bathroom floor: *dead frogs are considerably less
appealing than live ones.* A dead book doesn't move
you one way or another. It just leaves you cold. A live
book is the kind to find for yourself and children, a
fresh breath of life, nothing dead or dull or preserved
past its time. Whether it's a picture book, fiction, or
nonfiction, the book must be alive enough to grab
your attention and hold it. That's the main criterion.

Children's books are often full of good intentions,
but that doesn't make them good books. Indeed, some
of the worst books have the best intentions. Sweet and
preachy is a nauseating combination. The child who
is used to being preached at will more probably turn
off or wriggle away.

Good picture books are guaranteed not to cause
turning off or wriggling away. They will instead make
you want more good picture books. Picture books can
move as quickly as an action-packed novel with lots
of dramatic potential for reading aloud. Or they can
be a cross between painting and poetry, to be savored
slowly and looked at leisurely.

These days, adults and children alike are barraged
with images and sound. There is so much to see and
hear, no one really has much chance to look or listen.
Picture books are a chance to slow down and do both.

It's important, then, that the words sound smooth and natural, not choppy and artificial like the old Dick and Jane textbooks. It's important that the pictures, even in books for the *youngest*, look rich and inventive, not empty and superficial.

Picture books can range from illustrated songs, nursery rhymes, and identification, alphabet, and counting books for toddlers, to ethnic tales, folklore, and contemporary short fantasies or realistic stories for five- to seven-year-olds. In every good book the two elements of skill and originality will cause a contagious reaction. A good Halloween story, for instance, will be just as ingenious as a good costume—and just as important to the occasion. That's a handy thing to remember for party entertainment.

Old and young will smile in response to really funny pictures, or concentrate on really beautiful ones, or feel warm and secure with a cozy bedtime story, or sometimes get caught up in suspense. Children can teach adults a lot about looking at things because they take their time when they feel like it, whether it's putting on shoes or going to the store, and allow themselves to get sidetracked by interesting things. Sometimes it's enough to drive you crazy, but in relation to books, it's an advantage. Their only deadline is when they've finished exploring the book. And their instincts are right.

The best way to choose a picture book is to look— to stare. Take the tourist or art gallery gazer approach. Make your way to the library or bookstore sometime, child in tow, and look at all kinds of children's book illustration—paintings, drawings, collages, cartoons. It will soon be clear that the real trouble with poor quality pictures is that they all look alike. Good illustrators get right into the heart of the story and make it come alive with lines, colors, shapes, textures, patterns. Book designers frame those good illustrations in the right paper, space, print, margins, endpapers.

In any random selection of books what you see may be finely detailed or frantically cluttered, nicely simple or crudely unskilled, absorbing or dull, unusual or stereotyped, original or conventional, careful or sloppy, strong or heavy-handed, deepened or overstuffed. To some extent, what you like will be a matter of taste. People furnish their minds a lot like they furnish their rooms, with words and pictures that simply appeal to them.

One of the things that emerges as important in picture-book art is expressive characters. Characters don't have to be pretty; they can be *quirky;* they can offer something distinctive in the way of being human or animal. They can offer a change from Hollywood heroes or television-commercial heroines or cutesy-faced creatures that people used to think appropriate for a child. The faces children themselves make in a mirror are a clue to how far their imaginations can stretch to enjoy a different look!

The sweetness-and-innocence nostalgia, or what adults sometimes think *ought* to suit the state of childhood, can stand in the way of those urgent criteria of fresh art and living literature. When I was just out of graduate school and stuffed with the knowledge of what makes a good children's book, a teacher happened to request that the school library order multiple copies of the same edition of *Winken, Blinken, and Nod* I had grown up with. She wanted all her second graders to read it. I was delighted, but my supervisor looked at the book with horror. "We can't order that," she said. "Look at the pictures! There are much better editions available." Brushing aside the haze of nostalgia filming my eyes, I saw something I really wouldn't want to foist off on children. It was "cute" but flat, emotionless, and dull. The faces looked like a row of kewpie dolls. On second glance, I did not feel anything except a longing for a past of my own with which few modern children could connect. A child is *living* childhood, not remembering it, so that rosy glow of looking backward doesn't connect with their experience of reality.

Children feel strongly, and their books should live up to their emotional potential. What's more, their visual reaction precedes their verbal understanding. They *see* and know before they speak and know; a picture book, then, has a visual impact as important as its verbal impact. Since children will absorb the images they see, they shouldn't be cheated with a constant stream of boring, empty pictures. What they stare at does make an impression. Most people have had the experience of picking up a book or picture they had in childhood and feeling a kind of power in it because of its association with childhood impressions during a time when everything seems bigger and more wondrous than it does in later life. The resulting imprint can be either a piece of strong Sendak art or a weak, imitation-Disney cartoon. The richer the early diet of art, the more deep-rooted will be the child's appreciation of art later on. A lot of pleasure can grow from picture books, much of it depending upon the parents' choice.

There is a long and honorable tradition of artists who made art for children live up to the same standard as art for adults. Howard Pyle, Edmund Dulac, Arthur Rackham, Walter Crane, George Cruikshank, Randolph Caldecott, and Maxfield Parrish were not artists for children but simply *artists* who also illustrated for children. Their craft and vision were the best possible for any person who happened to look, and that is still the ideal picture-book illustration.

Good art doesn't have to exclude children's interests. Child appeal, that special way of looking at things from a ground level, is what gives picture-book art an extra special twist. In *Mr. and Mrs. Pig's Evening Out*, for instance, which is a classic updated battle between the good guys and the bad guys, the child's-eye view is very strong. What saves the whole story from being a tired replay of the wolf and the three little pigs is artist Mary Rayner's letting the young reader recognize, while the mother and father pig do not, that the baby-sitter is a wolf.

There is so much suspense and humor in the painting of that wolf knitting on the sofa with her hairy legs crossed, starting to feel a little *hungry*, and going to turn the *oven* on. Yet the book is no scarier than *The Three Little Pigs*; as in the folktales of old, everyone here knows these piglets are going to prevail. According to psychiatrists such as Bruno Bettelheim, it's even reassuring for children to have villains recognized and overcome. And again, like the tale of old, whatever moral exists is less important than the very dashing story. In general, the less a moral shows through, the better. Children know a sermon from a story and, like most people, prefer the story.

Of course, not all picture books are intended to be stories, and the occasional moral never hurt anybody. You never can tell, with frogs or books, what's going to turn out swimmingly. M. B. Goffstein's *Natural History*, for instance, is a beautifully crafted book that can inspire good discussion between child and adult, and it's like a sermon, or rather a poetically stripped-down statement of how our earth works: "Tiny grains of sand keep the powerful waters from flooding lands." Or sometimes our earth doesn't work: "Homeless dogs and cats are scared and lonely." And finally, how each of us can help it along: "So let us be like tiny grains of sand, and protect all life from fear and suffering! Then when the stars shine, we can sleep in peace, with the moon as our quiet night-light."

What keeps the text from being sentimental or over-generalized are the exact pictures, clean in line and understated in color, that speak directly to the child's experience of sharing resources with all things on earth—"ducks and singing birds and snakes and little minks." It's a relief to find some gentle antidote to overdoses of violent television cartoons. Our humane concerns and generalized social responsibility can be translated to our own children by starting small at home—reading aloud, for instance, about the experiences of others and talking over the idea that "every living creature is our brother and our sister, dearer than the jewels at the center of the earth."

The message that works without degenerating into a piece of propaganda is rare, though, and most of us would prefer hearing something entertaining, especially about ourselves. Books like Russell Hoban's *Bedtime for Frances* offer the truth of human behavior in disguise—in this case, the disguise of a badger family's life.

Here, Frances is having a hard time getting to sleep. She has been through the ritual glass of milk, piggy-back ride to bed, good-night kisses from Mother and Father, may-I-have-the-door-open request, long meandering song, finding a tiger in the room, finding a giant in the room, getting a piece of cake to quiet her hunger pangs, discovering a dangerous crack in the ceiling, attending to the forgotten toothbrush. Suddenly the curtains blow out in a peculiar way. The teddy bear is not much help.

"Maybe there is *something* waiting, very soft and quiet. Maybe it moves the curtains just to see if I am watching." She went into Mother and Father's room to tell them. They were asleep.

Frances stood by Father's side of the bed very quietly, right near his head.

She was so quiet that she was the quietest thing in the room. She was so quiet that Father woke up all of a sudden, with his eyes wide open.

When that sleeping Father raises one eyelid and says, "Umph!" together with a lot of other things that finally get Frances into bed, there's no question about who he really sounds like: every good-hearted, very tired fatl.er who has ever mumbled his children through their nighttime fears.

Similarly, Susan Jeschke's *Firerose* creeps close to human nature even though it's a fantasy. All of us feel at one time or another that we're different from everybody else by virtue of a large nose, short legs, fat stomach, triangular eyes, or some such odd feature. Firerose was born with a "delicately curled green tail." How her fortune-telling foster mother first rejects it, then accepts it, and finally returns it to its own young dragon makes a fine narrative background for the author's homely pencil sketches, which also serve to prove that imagination can bloom in black and white (and that funny-looking people can be lovable—a great comfort to many of us).

Jeschke pulls one of the favorite tricks of picture book fantasy, plunking something absurd right into the middle of an ordinary situation to see what happens. That is just the kind of uninhibited thinking children delight in and adults could benefit from. Margaret Mahy's *The Boy Who Was Followed Home* is another good example.

> One day a small, quite ordinary boy, called Robert, was coming home from school. He looked over his shoulder and there was a hippopotamus following him.

Robert was surprised and pleased—pleased because he had always liked hippopotami, and surprised because nothing like this had ever happened to him before.

When he got home the hippopotamus followed him up the steps and tried to come in at the door. Robert thought his mother would not like this, so he shooed it way.

It went and lay down in the goldfish pool on the lawn.

Things go from bad to worse, till the inevitably suitable but unexpected climax. Meanwhile, Steven Kellogg's illustrations have compounded the details of the dilemma. Lavender hippopotami crowd the elegant lawn, jostling each other and the beleaguered members of the household. One of them peers into a classroom filled with children in every memorable posture of mischief, boredom, and earnest endeavor. When a disreputable-looking witch is telephoned to solve the problem, she appears with an entourage of pastel-colored vermin and vipers. And the concluding surprise behind Robert, after forty-three hippopotami have finally been induced to slink away with reproachful looks, is a triumphant parade of glorious, golden-brown giraffes following him home the next day.

In this book's ending the pictures tell it all. In other cases, there is no text throughout. Wordless picture books are fun for children to pore over independently or make up their own words for. Raymond Briggs's *The Snowman* is the dream of a boy whose snowman has come alive, romped through his house with him, and swept him up for a ride through the night sky before his bittersweet awakening to the melting sun. The illustrations are arranged in comic-strip fashion but done with subtle colors and loving care. The same illustrator's *Father Christmas* is an all-time wordless favorite, showing a grouchy Santa puttering through his chores on the big day.

Though fantasy often creeps into picture books, sometimes the most beautiful are realistic. Aliki wrote and illustrated a book called *The Two of Them*, a poignant portrayal of the relationship between a girl and her grandfather. It starts at the very beginning:

> The day she was born, her grandfather made her a ring of silver and a polished stone, because he loved her already. Someday it would fit her finger.

And moves to the very end:

> She knew that one day he would die. But when he did, she was not ready, and she hurt inside and out.
> It was spring and she cut blossoms from his trees and gave them to him, and said, "Good night forever, Papouli," but he did not answer.

In between, their good times together unfold in such natural and complete postures that it is hard to believe so much of two lives has been distilled into twenty-six pages. The cycle of life and death and the immortality of ordinary people loving each other has been caught with a kind of shorthand wisdom and warmth that seldom graces so young a portrayal.

Such books give listeners a chance to talk about the death of an older person they're attached to, either in preparation for the fact or after it has happened. Perhaps open discussion can lead new generations out of the kind of irrational terrors that haunted a friend of mine who could not board an airplane because she was told as a child that her dying grandfather, whom she never saw again, had "gone for a ride in the sky." Many difficult subjects, from divorce to disabilities, have been presented for the better understanding of young children.

Any kind of factual information can be conveyed humanly, if not humorously, in picture-book form. Tomie de Paola's *Charlie Needs a Cloak*, for instance, teaches the rudiments of the wool-to-cloth process in a series of graphic jokes that pokes fun at both shepherd and sheep. The only creature that makes good is an inconsequential mouse that keeps nipping useful tidbits into his hole, a comment on life if ever there was one.

In the sprinkling of fantastic and realistic picture books mentioned so far, the art has been traditionally literal. There are wide and intriguing variations to look at. John Steptoe's story of a brother and sister, *My Special Best Words*, outlines his characters with the intensity of a neon sign in the rain. Leo and Diane Dillon, two-time Caldecott winners, illustrate African folktales with stylized designs and strikingly varied techniques. And filmmaker Gerald McDermott's abstract interpretation of folklore in his book

*Arrow to the Sun* has often found children more receptive than their elders.

Each of these illustrators has tailored an artistic vision to perfectly fit a story or text, to set it off and suit it and tell even more than the words already do. They have created an art that children and adults can share together in their own homes. Not many people take the time to go to a museum anymore; here is a museum that comes to you. Most people have watched their kids proudly bring home drawings and paintings which became fewer and fewer and finally stopped altogether. Sometimes the only images that flash by any of us, day after day, are the television screen and billboards. Some children don't know any other kinds of pictures exist. It's a relief to be able to show them something richer.

Picture-book art and literature are hard to talk about separately because they belong together by definition in a complementary and even symbiotic relationship; one cannot exist without the other. And small children should no more be swindled in literature than in art. They will use the words they hear, and they shouldn't be cheated of hearing and viewing the best.

The short story is one of the most difficult forms of literature, with a discipline all its own. How much harder to make it complex enough to be good, yet simple enough to be understood by a young child! The picture-book text must be pithier, developed more actively, more briefly, but just as believably as an adult short story. Folktales are ideal short stories for children because by their very nature they are pruned of any excess detail, right down to the bones of archetypal character and stark pattern of action.

Most modern stories, on the other hand, develop through details of dialogue and description, which must be selected with excruciating care and an eye for the truest, most vivid, pared-down, relevant language. These details should relate to a child's experience, although that is often broader than many adults assume. In *Tell Me a Mitzi*, author Lore Segal and artist Harriet Pincus joke about everything from parents to presidents. New York City in its grubby glory is revealed through the eyes of Mitzi and her brother Jacob. Theirs is an average family, the kind that succumbs to the common cold. You don't find too many fairy godmothers dealing with diaper changes, thermometers, and chicken soup.

The ideal short story can be funny or serious or sad, but, like the illustrations, should be moving one way or the other. It can be familiar or fantastic, but the characters must be as clear as close friends, the plot developed as naturally as day following night. Only hack writers will depend on artificial contrivances, or artificial language, to force a story along. Hackneyed writing is just as tiresome as hack art. Witness:

Billy Boll Weevil was an insect. He lived on a cotton farm. The farmer did not like Billy Boll Weevil. "Go!" he said. The farmer's wife did not like Billy Boll Weevil. "Go!" she said. The farmer's son did not like Billy Boll Weevil. "Go!" he said. The farmer's daughter did not like Billy Boll Weevil.

Guess what she said? After a tediously repetitious search for help, Billy Boll Weevil advises the farmer to plant peanuts and thereby becomes a local hero instead of a pest.

Children themselves think and articulate more imaginatively than that. A six-year-old I know suggested to her mother, who was grumbling about the cost of shoes, that somebody invent a pair that grew with your feet. The truth is that most kids have very inventive ideas. It takes a clever artist and original writer to live up to such naturally lively thoughts and actions.

Along with even the very youngest one- to four-year-olds, you can enjoy concept books—A B C, I.D. (identify the object), counting, and singing books, not to mention the simplest tales. Rosemary Wells has illustrated some board books for toddlers that tell stories of two rabbit siblings with just a few words to each page. She electrifies all of her books with wry humor and quick, quill-like penwork that makes anyone smile, especially over *Benjamin and Tulip*, the ultimate story of comeuppance. Reading these books out loud certainly beats mopping the kitchen floor while your children are overturning wastebaskets, testing each for edible objects and fighting over what they find, in the next room. The kitchen floor may stay dirty, but everyone will be in a better frame of mind, not to mention enriched artistically.

Toddlers can find rainy-afternoon relief looking at Aliki's rustic paintings for *Hush Little Baby* while you sing the song. It doesn't matter if you can't sing. Croak! Here we must move away from the aesthetic approach. Playing "This Little Pig Went to Market" and "Peek-a-Boo" shouldn't make you feel like a fool after the first time around. Once you get involved, you'll find it's not any worse than some of the television shows you expose your mind to and can be considerably more lively, given a few creative variations. In *Catch Me and Kiss Me and Say It Again*, Clyde and Wendy Watson have a verse for every occasion, from cutting the nails of spaghetti-fingered infants to changing diapers. Clyde Watson's magic incantations work like a charm for the very youngest of all, and her sister Wendy's sunny, funny-faced illustrations give everyday activities the aspect of a game.

This activity aspect is important in the development of young children's first interest in books. Starters need books that move in some way: illustration, detail, story action, silly sounds, word play, games, singing, or just pointing-and-naming possibilities. That's why the picture books of Dr. Seuss and Richard Scarry are so successful—they have a lively cinematic quality. Neither artist varies his style, which finally gets tedious, but each is an enduring attention-grabber, offering youngsters the kind of tidbits an inquisitive adult gets hooked on browsing through the encyclopedia or a favorite magazine. In fact, a picture encyclopedia is not a bad investment for a child just learning to talk. Or try books like Eve Rice's *Sam Who Never Forgets*, with a simple story line and lots of animals to name.

Art without action is sometimes lost on children. Most mood pieces amount to coffee-table juvenilia, beautiful but not quite balanced between aesthetic beauty and practical appeal. Sometimes they do work together well—as does Uri Shulevitz's *Dawn*—as a kind of retreat, but in general little children are not given to meditative books. They can tolerate a long text, such as Marianna Mayer's adaptation of *Beauty and the Beast*, if it has the kind of movement and emotions that Mercer Mayer has rippled through his accompanying illustrations. The Mayers' book will rivet five- to seven-year-olds and also give them, and any adults, art worth the attention.

Three- to five-year-olds, on the other hand, are more likely to appreciate books like Ivan Sherman's *I Do Not Like It When My Friend Comes to Visit*, a self-explanatory title if ever there was one, recognizably well-suited to an early stage of development. Fortunately, adults find it funny too, which always helps through the fiftieth reading.

The same wide variety appears in alphabet, counting, and concept books. Don't let the number of possibilities overwhelm you. Two- to five-year-olds need a clear-flowing arrangement of letters or numbers, as in Marcia Brown's *All Butterflies* or Roger Duvoisin's *A for the Ark*, while *Anno's Alphabet* catches the older eye with illusory twists in every drawing, and *Anno's Counting Book* is like a puzzle that unfolds the four seasons as well. Pages of *Hosie's Alphabet* (written and illustrated by Leonard Baskin) could be hung in a museum. *As I Was Crossing Boston Commons* (written by Norma Farber and illustrated by Arnold Lobel) is in fact sold in the Metropolitan Museum in New York. *Ape in a Cape* by artist Fritz

Eichenberg was one of the first ABC's with a sense of mischief; *Albert B. Cub and Zebra* is a complicated visual mystery by author-artist Anne Rockwell.

Any book can be made into a game of identification —the word spoken, the object pointed to—in an ongoing introduction to language, art, and bedtime. There is a whole world of variations: *Moja Means One* (Muriel and Tom Feelings) features an African setting; *One Old Oxford Ox* (Nicola Bayley), an English setting. There are concept books like Tana Hoban's *Opposites*, accompanied by fine photographs, and "helpful situation" books like Harlow Rockwell's *My Dentist, My Doctor*, and *My Nursery School*.

Books for babies can be made by sewing "pages" of plain heavy material, cut with pinking shears, together down one side and cutting out shapes of familiar objects (which can be traced from magazine pictures) out of other scraps and sewing them on the pages. Some material may even be printed already with dogs, horses, flowers, or other figures that can be cut out, sewn on, and labeled with laundry markers. You and the baby can name the figures and play rhyming lap games to match them, such as "Ride a Cock Horse to Banbury Cross" or "This Little Pig Went to Market."

Mother Goose, nursery rhyme, and nursery-tale books are innumerable. They are as old as childhood and seem to multiply like children. They've flourished in jungles, in streets, and now in print. They range from old-fashioned versions like Blanche Wright's *The Real Mother Goose* to modernistic ones like *Brian Wildsmith's Mother Goose*, from light-toned illustrations to dark-toned, from sensible to nonsensical, from ancient to current.

Illustrators such as Kate Greenaway from the nineteenth century still flourish alongside contemporary Japanese poster art on the picture-book shelf, a shelf that appears to stretch to every corner of the world in rhyme and prose. U.S., British, East and West European, Russian, Oriental, African, South American, and Australian nursery rhymes and tales all have found homes in picture books for young children.

Only a few are listed below. It is a matter of choice, a matter of stimulating the imagination with the richest books. The picture book you read—and so give—to a child can move your own eye and mind and heart.

## CHAPTER 4

### Spellbinders

FREEMAN, DON. *Corduroy* (4–6). Viking (hardcover); Puffin (paper).
A toy bear fears that missing a button on his overalls will prevent anyone from wanting to take him home.

GAG, WANDA. *Millions of Cats* (5–8). Coward-McCann (hardcover and paper).
A man and his wife long for one little cat—and end up with millions.

THE BROTHERS GRIMM. *Snow White and the Seven Dwarfs*, translated by Randall Jarrell, illustrated by Nancy Burkett (5–8). Farrar, Straus & Giroux.
Exquisite artwork brings to life this classic tale of "the fairest of them all."

HOBAN, RUSSELL. *Bread and Jam for Frances* (5–8). Harper & Row (hardcover and paper).
Only bread and jam will make this determined young badger happy.

KEATS, EZRA JACK. *The Snowy Day* (4–6). Viking (hardcover); Puffin (paper).
A boy shares his delight at seeing the winter's first snowfall.

MARSHALL, JAMES. *George and Martha* (5–8); Houghton Mifflin (hardcover and paper).
Two funny, affectionate hippopotami teach each other what caring and sharing are all about.

MCCLOSKEY, ROBERT. *Make Way for Ducklings* (5–8). Viking (hardcover); Puffin (paper).
A family of ducks makes its way through Boston as they search for a home—and create a commotion.

RAYNER, MARY. *Mr. and Mrs. Pig's Evening Out* (5–7). Atheneum.
When their baby-sitter turns out to be Mrs. Wolf in disguise, ten little piglets win a robust battle of wits.

REY, H. M. *Curious George* (5–8). Houghton Mifflin (hardcover and paper).
Curious George makes more mischief than a barrel of monkeys as he tries to find out about *everything*.

WELLS, ROSEMARY. *Benjamin and Tulip* (4–7). Dial (hardcover and paper).
After bugging a friend once too often, a raccoon gets her comeuppance.

### More Spellbinders

BEMELMANS, LUDWIG. *Madeleine* (5–8). Viking (hardcover); Puffin (paper).

BROWN, MARGARET W. *Goodnight Moon* (3–6). Harper & Row.

CREWS, DONALD. *Freight Train* (5–8). Greenwillow.

DE BRUNHOFF, JEAN. *Babar and His Children* (3–6). Random House.

KELLOGG, STEVEN. *The Mysterious Tadpole* (4–8). Dial (hardcover and paper).

SCARRY, RICHARD. *Richard Scarry's Best Word Book Ever* (4–8). Golden Press.

SEGAL, LORE. *Tell Me a Mitzi* (4–8). Farrar, Straus & Giroux.

SEUSS, DR. *The 500 Hats of Bartholomew Cubbins* (5–8). Vanguard.

WARD, LYND. *The Biggest Bear* (5–8). Houghton Mifflin (hardcover and paper).

WILDSMITH, BRIAN. *Brian Wildsmith's ABC* (5–8). Watts.

## This Kid Can't Read?
### Jumping from Picture Books to Older Literature

# 5

Reading is a doorway for some children, but for lots of others it's a stone wall. Before setting off into literature, you and your reading partners should be on free and equal footing in the reading realm.

I know the reading problem firsthand because I had to solve one. My daughter was not one of those whiz kids who taught herself to read at the tender age of three. She was one of those individuals, often labeled stubborn, who do things in their own sweet time. In the second grade she tested out at a first-grade reading level. She thought reading was hard; she got scared she'd fail at it; she decided to postpone the whole project. Fear is the first step down the road to failure. Her teacher was worried and beginning to suggest special tests for eyes, brain, perception, coordination, and digestion. The child seemed bright enough, but maybe something was the matter.

Panic. At first it seemed odd that *my child* wouldn't like to read. I had all these books I could hardly wait to share with her. On second thought, it made sense that a librarian/writer's child would have a complicated reaction to books. I just had to figure out what to do about it.

A lot of parents do. There are many reasons children don't read, but there are not too many ways to overcome them. The best cure is motivation, a book that hooks them. Children who can't read the first page of a geography textbook have been known to whiz through the *National Geographic*. Failures in the basal reading series may tackle airplane model instructions without a pause or problem.

To motivate a child one needs the motivating book, which usually requires a connection, like the French Connection—this one to be called the Adult Connection. An adult tracks down and gets hold of that Motivating Book and then leaves it, unobtrusive but also unavoidable, on the kitchen table. An adult who will read it out loud can clinch the deal. As the above-mentioned nonreader said once, "If you just read the first chapter, then I get interested."

British writer and critic John Rowe Townsend maintains that "a book is not a labor-saving device." He also says, "A reading child can be identified before conception." In other words a lot depends on the adult's attitude as well as the book's magic. The right combination of the two makes the best teaching tool possible.

Any interested adult will do. No special training is necessary, but patience helps. In my case, training was sometimes handy, but dealing with children and books on a personal level was a whole new learning experience from the professional. Instinct told me to lay off the tests until time and a couple of good books had had their chance. After all, everyone travels at his or her own pace. But I did start leaving irresistible books lying around the kitchen table—easy, funny, sensitive, secure books like Ursula Nordstrom's *The Secret Language* and Beverly Cleary's *Ramona the Pest* (more about this later), which hooked my nonreader.

The result of the laughter, tears, and companionship that she has found in books is "success" at reading: by the fourth grade she was testing at tenth-grade level. But the real reward is her habit of reading, thinking, feeling, articulating, writing, entertaining herself for hours at a time, experiencing other people's minds and lives through the looking glass of their writing.

This is not an isolated phenomenon, and it is not confined to worried writers' children. There have been reports ranging from unexpected responses of handicapped children—the most detailed is Dorothy Butler's *Cushla and Her Books*—to cases of whole schools "going book," as in districts of Pennsylvania that have a SQUIRT program. During the Super Quiet Undisturbed Individual Reading Time, everybody reads—children, teachers, clerical staff, principal, custodian. The phone in the secretary's office is off the hook. With adults practicing what they preach, any activity seems contagious. Kids will if you will.

As far as textbooks and teaching machines go, it doesn't make sense to achieve literacy and *then* give children literature, as educator Charlotte Huck pointed out, but to achieve literacy *through* literature. Nobody learns to swim on dry land, and most basal reading series, perhaps updated from Dick and Jane but still written to a prescribed formula, are a desert of nonliterature.

Here is the entire text of a typical recent book given to children learning how to read, with illustrations looking like a 1950s mail-order catalog. If this deadens your senses, just think how it must kill the interest of a restless new reader.

"When will it be my birthday?" asked Mary.
"Soon," said her father.
"Will my birthday come soon?" asked Mary.
"Soon," said her mother.
"I wish my birthday would hurry," said Mary.
"Will my birthday come soon?" asked Mary.
"It won't be long," said Grandfather.
"I wish my birthday would hurry," said Mary.
"There are just ten more days," said Grandmother.
"Will my birthday come soon?" asked Mary.
"Soon," said her teacher.
"I wish my birthday would hurry," said Mary.
"Just a few more days," said Father.
"I can't wait for my birthday!" said Mary.
"Just four more days," said her brother.
"Hurry up, birthday!" said Mary.
"My birthday is tomorrow," Mary said happily.

"Happy birthday, everybody!" shouted Mary. "My birthday hurried up. Now I wish it would slow down."

Read out loud, this sounds like someone chopping onions for an hour and a half. One six-year-old dubbed it the "worst book alive," but it's not really alive, and unfortunately, it's not really that unusual. It is quite often the kind of thing foisted on just such six-year-old children who trail groaning into the reading circle.

A dull book simply dulls the child and the adult, whereas a live-wire book keeps them both reading more. Reading is more than mechanics, it's magic. Emotional relevance is probably the biggest factor to a nonreader. Individually, emotional relevance can translate into anything from dogs to baseball cards, dollhouses to spooks. Combined with compelling writing and art, the vital interest factor is an absolute winner.

Sylvia Ashton-Warner couldn't find that kind of book when she was teaching New Zealand aboriginal children to read, so she let them whisper an important word to her. She wrote it down on a scrap of paper, which the next day was returned to her hand in tattered, moist shreds, but scrawled on a mind forever—"ghost," "mother," "afraid," "fight." Words like "the," "Dick," and "Jane" stopped those children cold, but they never faltered over the hard words they had asked for. Eventually they wrote their own textbooks with their own important words.

On the other hand, there is the period, often when

reading is just getting started and isn't solid yet, when the best tone seems to be light and low-key. It's hard enough to concentrate and get the sentences to run together correctly, much less figure out what's happening and what it all means. At that point, the funny and familiar seem to work best. The step backward from hearing complex stories read out loud to figuring them out with enough speed and ease not to lose track of the meaning can be discouraging.

Normally, the big crossover from listening to reading comes sometime during second to third grade. It can be earlier or later, but at some point the child has to jump from hearing and looking at picture books as a source of literature, to reading "chapter books" for independent enjoyment and school use. When children don't move into reading ease it eventually affects their education, work life, financial possibilities, and adult environment. Learning to read well determines a child's entire future, so those years from seven to nine are crucial.

The transition to reading ease is tough unless there's motivation, which points to the most important elements of fiction for children this age—plot and humor. Children will read to find out what happens and to laugh. This gets back to just which books it was that I left on the table for the reluctant reader—and the adult who's trying to help without dying of boredom. And that brings us to important names like Arnold Lobel and Beverly Cleary, who have made more children smile and read on than almost any other writer except Judy Blume, who for the most part comes a little later in the reading game.

Lobel's work is some of the best in a whole genre of beginning-to-read books, which have a simple, controlled vocabulary with a good story percolating through it and enough pictures to ease a formidable page full of print. Beginning-to-read books can be read aloud as picture books by an adult, but then they can be picked up and read independently by the listeners who want to get another crack at the story on their own. Their having read and liked the story will provide a push in the right direction. At best, children have been known to learn how to read this way without ever realizing it, which shortcuts a good deal of painful effort on everyone's part. At the very least, the easy words and appealing format of beginning-to-read books make a great practice field.

Lobel happens to have a gift for this elemental level of writing and drawing; he stays simple and sweet without getting corny. His stories and art almost always have humorous insight within easy reach of a little thought but can just as well hold their own at a literal level. His innate sympathy for small creatures extends throughout a humble world of frogs, toads, grasshoppers, mice, and owls, all with their own vanities, all drawn with earthy tones and detail and a gently mocking earnestness that win you over to regular visits.

Other authors and artists have added their own flair to the easy-reading genre. Crosby Bonsall and Syd Hoff broaden Lobel's plateau of amusement at the animal race to a plain of hilarity that includes a few funny-looking human characters as well. Regional flavor lifts some of the beginning-to-read books high above ordinary. *Squash Pie* (Wilson Gage and Glen Rounds) is a delectable tall tale with scratchy, country-set sketches and *Wiley and the Hairy Man* (Molly Bang) a spooky southern swamp tale with imaginative, moss-soft drawings. Any of these books could stand on their own as young literature, but their additional feature of reading ease makes them an invaluable starter for rising readers.

Just one reading size larger than beginner is the kind of story Beverly Cleary writes in *Henry Huggins, Ellen Tebbits,* and the Ramona books. Cleary captures the everyday world of families with a fine eye for detail and a memory like an elephant for exactly what it feels like to be young in school or home situations. Children recognize themselves instantly and adults are bounced back into their own pasts with the speed of a time machine: what it's like not to have one's sheep costume ready for the Christmas program, what it's like to stomp around in the rain on a pair of homemade tin-can stilts, how hard it is when a father loses his job and a child watches helplessly as parental tension mounts and the beloved cat Picky-Picky hungrily refuses to touch the cheapest brand of pet food but gnaws the Halloween pumpkin instead.

Each chapter is a complete episode, a satisfying beginning-middle-end in itself, easy to read and identify with. In staying true to her picture of perpetually normal family living, Cleary also pokes fun at adults. At one point, beleaguered Mr. Huggins, watching a spoiled young visitor litter his living room during a party, whispers into the air, "How much Kleenex in a box, anyway?" To which a thrifty guest replies matter-of-factly, "Two hundred and fifty sheets," precisely summarizing her own personality in one blow.

The trick with these books is to read the first chapter aloud together and involve children, then turn them loose. They can finish comfortably and go back to the same series for more. Cleary has built up that circle of security that adults look for in their escape reading, with a slightly more innocent ear for dialogue.

Of course, she is not the only writer who does this, but she has been doing it well for twenty years. There are plenty of variations to throw on the table for spice. Betty MacDonald's series of books about *Mrs. Piggle Wiggle* has something of the same perennial appeal. *The Enormous Egg* (Oliver Butterworth), *Henry Reed, Inc.* (Keith Robertson), and *Mr. Popper's Penguins* (Richard and Florence Atwater) are all surefire hits with a similar light, episodic quality.

My favorite is Thomas Rockwell's *How to Eat Fried Worms*, which makes people laugh out loud. It is the story of a bet between two boys that one will eat fifteen worms within fifteen days or forfeit fifty dollars. Billy is determined to do it, his rival to prevent him. The punch line, inevitably, is that after choking down the required number of worms in various desperate recipes, Billy starts to like them and just keeps cooking when the bet is won.

The transition between learning reader and learned reader is a hard stage to write for. It doesn't attract the number of writers who want to develop more complicated novels for older readers. Consequently, it's

59

hard to find really good books for the precarious readers of eight or nine. Quality and popularity do crop up hand in hand, however, even for that age group, and should be cherished all the more for the fires they can light under a reluctant reader. For many readers paperbacks are less intimidating than hardcover books. Most of the best children's books are available in paperback editions now, and often are within the price range of a weekly allowance, which gives youngsters a chance to make their own choices —a terrific stimulus to reading.

Just a word here, too, about "junk books" like Nancy Drew, that best-selling James Bond of the younger set and the old-fashioned equivalent of the "high interest/low vocabulary" productions being cranked out since America discovered its reading problem. Nancy Drew isn't a soaring achievement; nor are the Hardy Boys, Cherry Ames, comic books, etc. But everybody needs a break. It should be clear by now that quality counts, but few read at peak capacity all of the time. Quality has its limitations just like anything else.

In that period of crucial consolidation into reading ease, anything interesting counts. For a little relaxation and regression later on and right over the adult threshold, children and teenagers have a right to their own versions of junk, which they will find and cherish on their own without any help from adults, and, one hopes, without too much hindrance. Their junk will not require your support or participation; however, balancing junk with some high-class adventures in taste will.

My own reluctant reader, by the way, paid me back in kind. On the recommendation of a fellow reviewer, I passed along one of those transitional hookers, *The Secret in Miranda's Closet* (Sheila Greenwald). It is no great literary feat, the reviewer said, but it would keep a nine-year-old occupied. It did. Mine consumed it in one gulp and said the next day, quietly but with great determination, "Mom, *you better read this book.*" I took the hint and was startled to recognize a character remarkably, I might say *uncomfortably*, like myself— a loving but work-minded mother of a loving but doll-playing daughter who needed to be liberated from her mother's liberation. We discussed the book and its conflicts and agreed on some adjustments in my schedule that made my daughter's life a lot more comfortable. You just never know when you're going to have to follow your own advice, and where it's going to take you. My daughter and I were able to spend more time together, and collecting dollhouse furniture got to be a kind of hobby for both of us. It reminded me of the art of painted miniatures, and finally of literary miniatures, of children's books which, like the child herself, were small but no less beautiful for that.

## CHAPTER 5

### *Sure Hits*

BLUME, JUDY. *Tales of a Fourth Grade Nothing* (7–10).
Dutton (hardcover); Dell Yearling (paper).
Pete's got problems, not the least of which is a
two-year-old brother who's driving him crazy!

BUTTERWORTH, OLIVER. *The Enormous Egg* (8–11).
Little, Brown (hardcover); Dell Yearling (paper).
His hen lays a gigantic egg and Nate finds himself
the proud owner of—a dinosaur!

CLEARY, BEVERLY. *Ramona and Her Father* (8–12).
Morrow (hardcover); Dell Yearling (paper).
When Mr. Quimby loses his job, daddy's girl
Ramona tries to help, and the results are hilar-
ious.

EASTMAN, P. D. *Are You My Mother?* (6–8). Beginner.
An easy, light-hearted story about a baby bird
who searches for his mother.

LOBEL, ARNOLD. *Frog and Toad Are Friends* (5–8).
Harper & Row (hardcover and paper).
Five exhilarating stories about a frog, a toad, and
their happy loving friendship.

MACDONALD, BETTY. *Mrs. Piggle Wiggle* (5–8). Lippincott (hardcover and paper).
Mrs. Piggle Wiggle may look a little peculiar—
but she knows some amazing ways to make children behave.

MINARIK, ELSE. *A Kiss for Little Bear* (5–8). Harper &
Row (hardcover and paper).
The kiss that Grandmother sends to Little Bear

is carried on its way by a hen, a frog, and a cat—
and that one little kiss leads to love.

ROCKWELL, THOMAS. *How to Eat Fried Worms* (8–10).
Watts (hardcover); Dell Yearling (paper).
Ten-year-old Billy hopes that worms can be deli-
cious because he's just made a bet that he'll eat
fifteen!

SOBOL, DONALD. *Encyclopedia Brown's Record Book
of Weird and Wonderful Facts* (8–12). Delacorte
(hardcover); Dell Yearling (paper).
The popular ten-year-old detective presents his
own collection of wild and amazing facts.

WILLIAMS, JAY. *Danny Dunn* series (8–11). McGraw-
Hill (hardcover); Archway (paper).
Action and excitement are the hallmarks of this
series about a budding scientist, his friends, and
their adventures.

### More Sure Hits

ATWATER, FLORENCE and RICHARD. *Mr. Popper's Penguins* (9 & up). Little, Brown (hardcover); Dell
Yearling (paper).

BYARS, BETSY. *The Midnight Fox* (9 & up). Viking
(hardcover); Puffin (paper).

CORBETT, SCOTT. *The Great McGoniggle's Key Play*
(8 & up). Atlantic Little, Brown (hardcover); Dell
Yearling (paper).

DRURY, ROGER. *The Champion of Merrimack County*
(9 & up). Litle, Brown (hardcover); Dell Yearling
(paper).

GAGE, WILSON. *Squash Pie* (5–8). Greenwillow (hardcover); Dell Yearling (paper).

LINDGREN, ASTRID. *Pippi Longstocking* (9–12). Viking (hardcover); Puffin (paper).

PARISH, PEGGY. *Amelia Bedelia* (5–8). Harper & Row (hardcover); School Book Service (paper).

ROBERTSON, KEITH. *Henry Reed, Inc.* (9–12). Viking (hardcover); Dell Yearling (paper).

LOUISE FITZHUGH

## *The Big Tomato—Fiction for Older Children*

# 6

Once, in the throes of writing a book, I lettered two reminders to myself. One three-by-five card neatly said "Patience," and the other, "Magic." They were the two ingredients I thought I needed for working on a novel, and for months they were taped to the wall above my desk.

One day I sat down to the typewriter and saw that my ten-year-old had added a sign right in the middle of the other two. It was a much bigger piece of paper with a neat circle on it colored red, and underneath it the words "Big Tomato." Suddenly the light dawned and I realized that Big Tomato was a much better symbol for writing than "Patience" or "Magic."

First of all, it was not abstract but concrete, which

is a mark of good fiction. Secondly, it was not colorless but vivid, like good writing. Thirdly, it was a common everyday detail, not a grandiose scheme; and grandiose schemes can only be built upon common everyday details. Finally, a tomato is, in its own way, something of a miracle. The same could be said of a good novel.

A National Book Award winner defined novels as being "full of people running around doing things to themselves and each other." The novel is not necessarily realistic, but it is *real*, like a big tomato. Even fantasy must be real, consistent. Magic must be a world that works.

People often think of children's fantasy, for instance, as involving sweet little fairies tiptoeing through the tulips. J. R. R. Tolkien in *The Lord of the Rings*, Ursula Le Guin in *A Wizard of Earthsea*, Susan Cooper in *The Dark Is Rising*, and Madeleine L'Engle in *A Wrinkle in Time* have all disproved that myth with their monumental series. In fact, fantasy is one of the most difficult forms of fiction that can cross the age barrier from young to old. Those tulip fairies are a long way from the high art that fantasy has become. It is not a genre with an automatic appeal to all children, but a special literature with its own strict rules, exactly right for *some* children and *some* adults, just as other people prefer realistic fiction or mysteries.

The more fantastic a piece of fiction is, the harder the writer must work to make it believable. *Beauty, A Retelling of the Story of Beauty and the Beast*, by Robin McKinley, is a 247-page juvenile novel that details the characters, setting, and action of the old fairy tale so clearly that a reader is forced to consider it as a real situation. Even the magic of the Beast's castle has been characterized into two invisible gossipy ladies-in-waiting who insist on Beauty's dressing elegantly much against her will. Beauty herself is no victim, but a stubborn, self-educated tomboy whose good looks are acknowledged only at the end of the book, after her inner value and intelligence have already endeared her. The Beast, too, takes on a complicated aspect of being irresistibly forceful and sadly vulnerable at the same time. The love that grows between the two has captured almost everyone old enough to read the book and not too old to harbor romantic dreams. It is an ideal novel for young adolescents and adults to share because, given a bent for well-grounded fantasy, they will enjoy it equally.

In dealing with younger children's fiction, whether fantasy or realism, you're up against the requirement of brief development again. Long pages of indulgent description or unadulterated intricacies of characterization without benefit of action will just draw a yawn. Plot is simply more compatible with a child's concentration span than elaborate style, but that is no excuse for not developing the best possible style and characters, along with a gripping plot. The details have to be chosen with selective self-discipline, but those very limitations, like a sonnet form, are a challenge for a good writer. Brevity, after all, is the soul of wit, and some of the best descriptions are brief caricatures, like this opening from Russell Hoban's *How Tom Beat Captain Najork and His Hired Sportsmen.*

Tom lived with his maiden aunt, Miss Fidget
Wonkham-Strong. She wore an iron hat, and took
no nonsense from anyone. Where she walked the
flowers drooped, and when she sang the trees all
shivered.

In novels, as in picture-book writing and art, it is
freshness that counts. Children—or people in general
—are deluged with the ordinary, the well-meant but
mummified, the TV-dinner titles. What's really exciting is fiction that *has* to be read because it *had* to be
written, not because it *ought* to have been written.
The idea of it was just too funny or sad not to over-
flow. And when it overflowed, it was channeled by
skillful writing.

Sometimes it comes as a big surprise that everyone
who knows children can't write a children's book. Not
even imagination is enough. Good intention is a
wonderful thing, but good intention without the
spark of inspiration isn't much at all, and inspiration
without writing skill is nothing.

The skills of fiction are the same for adult and
children's books. A plot can be suspenseful or inevitable, but there needs to be some element of surprise
in its unfolding. Nobody wants a predictable plot,
because it's pretty dull going. The same goes for
characters. No two people are alike; yet in children's
books a stereotyped character—a hero or villain with
no distinguishing characteristics or surprises—is often
allowed to pass as a mouthpiece for a writer's message.

Children's literature is particularly susceptible to

delivering messages through characters and situations. A message is not the same as a theme, or an idea that emerges from real, unique characters as they evolve their story. It is the characters who must shape the plot, theme, tone, style, and setting—or the book will not be convincing, but hollow. Caricatures can heighten comedy and archetypes deepen folklore, but stereotypes will flatten fiction.

In that old favorite Nancy Drew by Carolyn Keene, for instance, there's suspense, but it's hollowed out by hero/villain descriptions like this in *Password to Larkspur Lane*: "Ned Nickerson, who was tall and handsome, grinned"; or, "She studied the husky, broadshouldered man. He had heavy brows, deep-set eyes, and a cruel mouth." And that's about all we ever know of either character. Suspense is only part of a story. It is the human spirit of the book that our own human spirits respond to, that moves us and makes us care.

One of my touchstone characters in modern realistic children's fiction is Harriet the Spy. She is the one who broke through a tradition of children who were good all the time. She fluctuates as we all do from high to low to high again, from lovable to obnoxious, and back again. When she first appeared, adults thought her spying was controversial, but children immediately recognized her as one of themselves, yet different from anyone else. One of her idiosyncrasies is tomato sandwiches; another is practicing what it would feel like to be an onion. She is unique. There will never be another Harriet who loves tomato sandwiches and rolls around on the floor like an onion. It is these specific twists that make a good characterization for adult books or children's books.

Individualized characters generate their own problems and find their own solutions. The problems may vary from defying a comfortable school clique to facing a concentration camp. The solutions may range from accepting the decrees of society to suicide. All these problems have appeared in children's novels. If the characters are original, the plot has a chance to be. But plot involves the further techniques of storytelling—a tight movement from beginning to middle to end. Plot is the great spellbinder, the finding out what happens.

There is a wonderful passage in John Irving's adult novel *The World According to Garp*. It describes a publisher's infallible system for predicting that a book will be popular. Nobody knows that he gives the manuscript in question to a woman who cleans his office and who hates to read. If she finishes it, he knows it will be a winner.

> "If you hated it, why'd you read it, Jillsy?" John Wolf asked her.
> "Same reason I read anythin' for," Jillsy said. "To find out what *happens*."
> John Wolf stared at her. ". . . So you read it to find out?" John Wolf said.
> "There ain't no other reason to read a book, is there?" Jillsy Sloper said. . . . "It feels so true," she crooned, making the word *true* cry like a loon over a lake at night. . . . "A book's true when you

can say, 'Yeah! That's just how damn people *behave* all the time.' *Then* you know it's true,"
Jillsy said.

Like Jillsy Sloper, children and many other people
(if the truth were known) will sit still only so long for
descriptions of psychological complexity. They want
to know what happens next, and they want it to ring
true. Endings in folklore may be predictable, though
there is suspense in a higher and higher accumulation
of events that up the ante to a climactic, satisfying
conclusion. The events and endings of realistic fiction,
however, must be more unexpected, the way our own
lives are.

The heroine of Bette Greene's *Summer of My German Soldier* winds up in a reform school as punish-
ment for showing moral compassion. She is a southern
Jew who during World War II helps an escaped German prisoner of war, one of the few people in her
life who has been kind to her, in an act which the
rest of her society regards as criminal. Because the
writer took such care in building a real character
through unique details, natural dialogue, and carefully chosen scenes, the reader experiences Patty Bergen's personal agony of being rejected by parents and
peers from whom she desperately wants acceptance
and approval. And because of being so involved in
her as a real person, the reader cares deeply that she
is experiencing the most painful kind of alienation in
what adds up to a devastating ending.

Because the characters and plot have held true, the
theme emerges powerfully, forcing us to ask: What

is justice, personal and social? What place does love really have in a society riddled with prejudice? Who are society's real villains and who are its heroes—behind all the labels? How does one know what is right and how does one find the courage or will or desperation to do it? If Patty Bergen had been popular and "well-adjusted," would she have valued a lowly black servant as her best friend the way she did, or was that a function of her need as a problem child? You just don't find this kind of plot or character or theme in Nancy Drew. That's where many children are missing out.

The same depth can be found in fantasy, science fiction, mystery, comedy, historical fiction. It can be found in realistic stories of families, friends, and their survival against the odds of war or peace, natural or man-made environments. The world should not be boiled down to a thin broth of concepts for children. It is daring for writers to touch the sparks of reality and fantasy in a child's mind, which ranges from narrow experience to wide-open possibilities. The presentation or the technique can be simple, but the vision behind it has to be rich. It has to be as complex as the world is and as people are. That takes a lot of mastery—technical footwork. It takes a lot of work to let the complexity of things, or even hints of the complexity of things, show through a simple presentation.

A plot that develops out of well-realized characters will have a logical force that gives the book a natural urgency children and adults respond to and remember. A plot that is imposed on characters, in which the author as well as the reader are not surprised by unplanned twists, makes a contrived book; and artificial contrivance is the greatest plague in children's literature. It mars fiction, nonfiction, poetry, and picture books alike. It accounts for fake dialogue, false transitions, and patronizing information. Books should grow naturally, not be forced.

Fiction does not work with the abbreviated conventions of folklore. In fiction as in life, people have many sides to their characters. Even in a fantasy of good versus evil, such as *The Lord of the Rings*, Tolkien's lowest character, Gollum, is more poignant for the flashes of goodness that make us sympathetic enough to grieve for his loss to the side of the good.

The writer who has insight into the human condition and who has patience to probe it in fiction can move any reader beyond problems and solutions into the human realm. Such a writer may be able to pull off a good book for children. He or she does not try to give all the answers. One of the hardest things for adults to acknowledge to children is that we don't have all the answers.

Liberal and conservative thinkers can present points of view which do not amount to literature. The intention to teach a lesson or give a sermon can often overwhelm children's novels. Intention should be generated by the story, not the story by intention.

Larry Callen is a case in point. He writes a good story. In *Sorrow's Song*, one of a series about the mythical southern town of Four Corners, the heroine, Sorrow Nix, is mute and feels caged by her inability to speak. She identifies strongly with an injured whooping crane that a number of people are trying to trap. There is the greedy Zoo Man, who collects animals. There's John Barrow, who collects money from the Zoo Man to catch the crane. And there are the Sweet brothers, who recall the cranes of their youth as tasting better than turkey. Through the efforts of Sorrow Nix and her good friend Pinch Grimball, the bird is finally set free. In fact the friendship of the two children itself epitomizes Callen's compassion in dealing with nature, both human and animal. Callen has a simple, humorous way of pinning down the differences between wild and tame without pounding home his point.

One editor calls writing fiction the slow art of revelation. Writers want so badly to *tell* a reader—especially a child—what's what, but that won't work. Writing fiction means making the reader not just listen politely but *live through* the action along with the characters that have been slowly revealed, just the way people get to know other people, one glimpse at a time, with the future of the person or event unknown and the message left up to the reader's own discovery. Does an adult book need a moral? It is a rich portrayal of human beings and what happens to them, which is the reason so many people have enjoyed reading it. Children deserve the same kind of enjoyment in their fiction.

Fiction extends just as far as imagination and skill can take it. Today children's fiction is going farther and farther, now that writers have grasped it as a real literature worth their best energy and interest. An adult friend of mine read and loved *Summer of My German Soldier* without knowing that it was a

74

novel published for children. The good novel for children should be just as good as the good novel for adults, but with the extra requirement of being relevant to the child's special experience. That's not easy to do, and of course it's not always done. Children's books are no more perfect than adults'. But it's something to shoot for, to remember in looking for a good novel. The same thing that makes Joseph Heller's *Catch-22* move adults makes *My Brother Sam Is Dead*, by James and Christopher Collier, move children and adults. Both books make the tragic ironies of war seem real through a carefully built, slowly revealed story. There are no shortcuts in writing for children.

From the examples of good juvenile fiction so far, it should be clear that no subject is off limits in this field anymore. Fiction ranges from treating terrible problems to inventing idyllic mood pieces. Characters may be raped and murdered, or they may simply have trouble picking out the right birthday present for a parent. They may be lost, deserted, "tessered" to a different time on a distant planet, or determined to learn how to cook. They may be giant chickens, mentally or physically handicapped children, genius detectives, or opera-singing crickets.

It's an open season on children's books. This is partly what makes them so interesting to some adults, and partly what makes them disturbing for others. The controversies will crop up in a later chapter, because they are an issue separate from quality.

Quality itself has many faces. One outstanding writer for children is Virginia Hamilton, who wrote the multi–award-winning *M. C. Higgins, the Great* and has experimented richly in each of her books, including a stream-of-consciousness narrative in *Arilla Sundown*. This may be an experimental edge that some children find baffling, but her work is important in opening up the way for future writers and their techniques and ideas. Just as important is the way she explores the black experience with humane insight rather than political self-consciousness.

The best-selling author Judy Blume, by contrast, is a very different kind of experimental writer, one who ventures into areas that some adults consider controversial but that children recognize as their common concerns. Her style is simple and smooth—mostly dialogue or a kind of first-person conversation with the reader that's as easy and accessible as watching television.

Blume's great talent is remembering her childhood secrets and reaching the juvenile majority who have the same secrets. She captures the desperately important trivia of growing up, of the most common concerns: Who likes me and who doesn't? Am I too fat? Why do Mom and Dad fight? *Are You There, God? It's Me, Margaret* is certainly one of the truest pictures of an ordinary suburban preadolescent worrying her way toward a place in the universe—a universe defined by family, friends, and getting her period. What could be more natural?

The one and only limitation of an exclusive diet of Blume's books is the sameness of experience. To date, her books circle a certain kind of average-modern-suburban problem. As a vivid writer, Blume deals realistically and truthfully with these concerns, but

76

her readers look into a roomful of themselves. That's not so much of a problem of Blume as of her self-limiting audience. Many children's horizons are never expanded to possibilities broader than their own psyches, to problems as different as hunger or home-lessness or war or even true peculiarity. There is in-stead just the sense of resolving personal difficulties, without much of the adventure a life might hold. The confessional tone of modern middle-class characters in a materialistically airtight world doesn't always make clear the difference between small details and petty details. But that is a reflection of the times, not of one author who is accurately reflecting those times.

Between the two extremes of "experimental" and "popular" stand writers like Scott O'Dell, who in *Island of the Blue Dolphins* creates an unusual but riveting saga of a Northwest Native American girl who remains on an island to find her brother when her people flee a hostile tribe. Her Robinson Crusoe–type experience is echoed in the resourcefulness of the heroine of *Julie of the Wolves*, by Jean George, about an Eskimo girl making her way alone across the North Slope of Alaska. These are both well-written and popular adventure stories.

Good writing and popular appeal can be found in every imaginable children's book setting, from a mid-western foster home to an underground Paris subway, from British garden to Greek mountainside, or beyond to the exploration of outer and inner space. Readers can pick whatever is most relevant and appealing. Fiction for children has come of age.

This is not to say that only new titles are good titles.

Before the "realistic revolution" of the early sixties set in, children's books followed a pattern of traditional values. The problems that came up in these books were not just coped with but triumphantly resolved. Many of the earlier books are dated now, but some still work well. They are innocent of the changing times, yet fundamentally knowing in a way that children sense and respond to. Eleanor Estes' *The Moffats* and Marguerite Henry's *Misty of Chincoteague* radiate a strong sense of warmth and security, a kind of commonplace happiness of growing up that some children may never have but still look for, no matter what their ages.

Not knowing the exact age range for which a book is appropriate, by the way, shouldn't worry a participating adult too much. It's just a matter of finding a book with plenty of room for a growing mind. Although the recommended lists suggest an age range for each title, individual children vary so much in abilities and interests that their involvement may tend toward books much higher or lower than any book's intended audience. What I've tried to get at here is quality in fiction. *The same quality holds true for any age book.* That is the central idea of children's literature: quality can crop up for every age from preschool to young adult.

It is true, on the other hand, that there are dominant concerns special to each age group, and the writer who can articulate these in a universal way has a rare talent. That is what makes E. B. White so well-loved; in *Charlotte's Web*, a story of friendship, a pig's understanding of a spider's death evokes responses on many levels.

The complexity of children's fiction ranges from the childlike antics of animal friends, such as those in *A Toad for Tuesday* by Russell Erickson, to young adult dramas like Paul Zindel's *The Pigman* in which two teenagers chronicle their part in the death of an old man who has become their friend. A mystery can be on the simple, funny picture-book level of Harry Allard's *Bumps in the Night*; or show a sophisticated Mark Twain sparkle as does Richard Peck's skillfully crafted *The Ghost Belonged to Me*; or carry the old-fashioned adventurous flavor of Sherlock Holmes as does Robert Newman's *Case of the Baker Street Irregulars*. An adult friend of mine was hooked into a lifelong habit of mystery reading by an early acquaintance with the *Freddy the Detective* pig series by Walter Brooks.

There are some ages when children do have special reading needs, in particular when they are just consolidating their skills. But once past that barrier, their reading depends on their interest, which may depend on adult interest. There is always one sure route around age categories—reading aloud. It's emotionally satisfying and leads the way to books a child will love reading alone.

## CHAPTER 6

### *Stories to Grow On*

BABBITT, NATALIE. *Tuck Everlasting* (8 & up). Farrar, Straus & Giroux (hardcover); Bantam (paper).
Winnie stumbles upon a mysterious family and their remarkable secret—the Tucks have found the source of everlasting life. But is it a blessing or a curse?

BLUME, JUDY. *Are You There God? It's Me, Margaret* (8 & up). Bradbury (hardcover); Dell Yearling (paper).
Twelve-year-old Margaret has lots of questions about growing up and learns to answer them herself.

BOND, MICHAEL. *A Bear Called Paddington* (6–9). Houghton Mifflin (hardcover); Dell Yearling (paper).
The endearing bear has a special gift for getting into all kinds of trouble.

BROOKS, WALTER R. *Freddy the Detective* (8–12). Knopf (hardcover); Dell Yearling (paper).
A clever pig sets out to solve some mysterious problems on the Bean farm where he lives.

FITZGERALD, JOHN D. *The Great Brain* (9–14). Dial (hardcover); Dell Yearling (paper).
Ten-year-old Tom Fitzgerald, the shrewdest con artist west of the Mississippi, gets in and out of trouble through a series of schemes.

GREENE, BETTE. *Summer of My German Soldier* (12 & up). Dial (hardcover); Bantam (paper).
A German prisoner of war hides in a small Ar-

kansas town during World War II, and nobody knows except a young Jewish girl.

KONIGSBURG, ELAINE. *From the Mixed-Up Files of Mrs. Basil E. Frankweiler* (8–12). Atheneum (hardcover); Dell Yearling (paper).

Claudia knows she has to run away, but grubby hideouts are not her style. The Metropolitan Museum of Art has all the elegance she wants—and much, much more.

L'ENGLE, MADELEINE. *A Wrinkle in Time* (10 & up). Farrar, Straus & Giroux (hardcover); Dell Yearling (paper).

There is only one way for Meg to rescue her missing father—by passing through another time dimension and depending on the power of love.

O'DELL, SCOTT. *Island of the Blue Dolphins* (10 & up). Houghton Mifflin (hardcover); Dell Yearling (paper).

Nature becomes both friend and enemy to a young Indian girl as she struggles to survive on a deserted island.

PINKWATER, D. MANUS. *Lizard Music* (8 & up). Dodd, Mead (hardcover); Dell Yearling (paper).

A contemporary fantasy shot through with absurdity and fun about a boy and his lizard.

### More Stories to Grow On

CONFORD, ELLEN. *The Luck of Pokey Bloom* (9–12). Little, Brown (hardcover); Archway (paper).

DANZIGER, PAULA. *The Cat Ate My Gymsuit* (11–15). Delacorte (hardcover); Dell Laurel-Leaf (paper).

ESTES, ELEANOR. *The Moffats* (9–12). Harcourt Brace Jovanovich (hardcover and paper).

HAMILTON, VIRGINIA. *M. C. Higgins, the Great* (12 & up). Macmillan (hardcover); Dell Laurel-Leaf (paper).

McCLOSKEY, ROBERT. *Homer Price* (8–13). Viking (hardcover); Puffin (paper).

NORTON, MARY. *The Borrowers* (8 & up). Harcourt Brace Jovanovich (hardcover and paper).

PECK, RICHARD. *The Ghost Belonged to Me* (12 & up). Viking (hardcover); Avon (paper).

RODGERS, MARY. *Freaky Friday* (10 & up). Harper & Row (hardcover and paper).

SELDEN, GEORGE. *A Cricket in Times Square* (7–12). Farrar, Straus & Giroux (hardcover); Dell Yearling (paper).

SHARP, MARGERY. *The Rescuers* (12 & up). Little, Brown (hardcover); Dell Yearling (paper).

## *The Life of Rhyme—Poetry and Folktale Collections for Children*

# 7

*Liar liar*
*Pants on fire*
*Nose as long*
*As a telephone wire*

Kids have probably been chanting that, or something like it, since dinosaurs strolled through the playground. Rhyming is as natural as climbing in early childhood. But for some reason a lot of people tune out poetry as they get older, probably because nobody goes around talking in iambic pentameter. Still, it's true that you can't say anything much more briefly than a poem or folktale says it, nor catch a fact or feeling much more expressively. Heard over and over, rhymed lyrics are almost unforgettable—witness popular songs and television commercials. Unfortunately, poetry cannot be read fast and therefore doesn't fit into the modern pace of things. That leaves poetry for those of us who read slowly, either through choice or necessity.

Being a misfit has its own rewards. For me, even newspaper articles require thought, so there are some days I really study the world and some days I don't even have time to glance down its columns. This makes for an uneven but carefully pondered universe. You can never know everything anyway; you might as well know something thoroughly. Take this simple fact, stated concisely in *The Poetry Troupe*, edited by Isabel Wilner.

> *For every evil under the sun*
> *There is a remedy, or there is none.*
> *If there be one, try and find it.*
> *If there be none, never mind it.*

Such good advice is hard to come by even in prose. It reminds me of the graffiti in a city park bathroom along my favorite jogging route:

> *Those who know me*
> *know me well.*
> *Those who don't*
> *can go to hell.*

The more often I read it, the more it strikes me as a succinct article of truth, a truth within easy grasp of either adult or child. It more or less rings in the mind for miles, keeping my heart up no matter how slow my pace may look to the public. It all goes to prove how poetry can boost the humblest activities of daily living.

As the critic Northrop Frye said in *The Educated Imagination*, "Poetry is not irregular lines in a book, but something very close to dance and song, something to walk down the street keeping in time to." Or jog down the trail keeping time to. Or do the dishes by. Or jump rope on the playground with. That rhythmic action of poetry is one of the things that arrests children's attention; it fills their own restless need for activity. The words of a poem, like children, must *move*. Those words also play with each other in sound patterns. Take this observation of nature by Ray Fabrizio from *Magic Lights and Streets of Shining Jet*:

> *Rabbits have fur*
> *And also more rabbits*
> *and it is a habit.*
>
> *A habit is something you are doing*
> *Over and over again*
> *Because you are liking it*
> *When you have it.*
>
> *A habit of rabbits is having more.*
> *First there is a rabbit with fur*
> *and you have it.*
> *But soon there are more.*

*Soon they are having more rabbits*
*Over and over again and liking to do it*
*And then it is a habit*
*And rabbits really have it.*

Fabrizio's poem fills the ears like a tipsy jumprope rhyme and brings to mind an important maxim of poetry that many people overlook: it doesn't have to be serious, it just has to be good.

Little children chant almost instinctively, as every tired parent knows. Shel Silverstein has a firm grasp on the efficacy of nonserious poetic statements. There's a swarm of them in *Where the Sidewalk Ends*:

*Oh, if you're a bird, be an early bird*
*And catch the worm for your breakfast plate.*
*If you're a bird, be an early bird—*
*But if you're a worm, sleep late.*

Or

*A hippo sandwich is easy to make.*
*All you do is simply take*
*One slice of bread,*
*One slice of cake,*
*Some mayonnaise,*
*One onion ring,*
*One hippopotamus,*
*One piece of string,*
*A dash of pepper—*
*That ought to do it.*
*And now comes the problem . . .*
*Biting into it!*

86

One poem for breakfast, one poem for lunch, both guaranteed to interfere with a sulk and improve disposition if not appetite. And here's one I picture for sunset, when the day's responsibilities melt away into the freedom of evening:

> *There is a place where the sidewalk ends*
> *And before the street begins,*
> *And there the grass grows soft and white,*
> *And there the sun burns crimson bright,*
> *And there the moon-bird rests from his flight*
> *To cool in the peppermint wind.*
>
> *Let us leave this place where the smoke blows*
>     *black*
> *And the dark street winds and bends.*
> *Past the pits where the asphalt flowers grow*
> *We shall walk with a walk that is measured*
>     *and slow,*
> *To the place where the sidewalk ends.*
>
> *Yes, we'll walk with a walk that is measured*
>     *and slow,*
> *And we'll go where the chalk-white arrows go,*
> *For the children, they mark, and the children,*
>     *they know*
> *The place where the sidewalk ends.*

Unless you can visualize the possibility of a hippopotamus sandwich or a place where the sidewalk ends, it will be impossible to appreciate the world of simple everyday phenomena translated into the marvels of verse.

Whether the poetry is lyric, narrative, epic, romantic, balladic, humorous, or nonsensical, whether it moves in regular metrical or free verse patterns, whether it rhymes or doesn't, it must speak of something you recognize. So much meaning can be stored in an image that summons hundreds of unstated associations. The image should be *fresh*, too. "And there the sun burns crimson bright, / And there the moon-bird rests from his flight / To cool in the peppermint wind." What a swirl of color sensations that is, compared to a stale cliché like "red as a rose."

There are two important things to remember about poetry: the first one is that it's fun to read aloud, which makes it ideal to share with children. The other is that some unusual image, some word surprise is bound to catch you up short and cause a sudden veering off the common course of thought. In the following poems, for instance, two reptiles make the same cogent point, one less elaborately than the other. Valerie Worth's "Toad" from *More Small Poems* seems simple.

*When the flowers*
*Turned clever, and*
*Earned wide*
*Tender red petals*
*For themselves,*

*When the birds*
*Learned about feathers,*
*Spread green tails,*
*Grew cockades*
*On their heads,*

*The toad said:*
*Someone has got*
*To remember*
*The mud, and*
*I'm not proud*

The word "earned" is such a surprise, much more exciting than "got" would have been, for instance, and echoing the sound of "turned" and "learned" without becoming singsong about it. But the best surprise is the toad's crusty self-evaluation, which casts shadows on the pride of others without sounding proud itself—all in a simple but choice comment of eleven final words perfectly suited to the character. The flowers, the birds, and the toad have all been seen in an entirely new way. By sleight of language Worth has let us in on her vision. Both the words and the idea are simple, yet unusual. It would take an older child to understand the ironies of the next poem by Hyacinthe Hill from *Straight on Till Morning,* and perhaps only in context of discussion with an adult.

*Rebels from Fairy Tales*

*We are the frogs who will not turn to princes.*
*We will not change our green and slippery skin*
*for one so lily-pale and plain, so smooth*
*it seems to have no grain. We will not leave*
*our leap, our spring, accordion. We have*
*seen ourselves in puddles, and we like*
*our grin. Men are so up and down, so thin*
*they look like walking trees. Their knees seem stiff,*

*and we have seen men shooting hares and deer.*
*They're queer . . . they even war with one another!*
*They've stretched too far from earth and natural*
*  things*
*for us to admire. We prefer to lie*
*close to the water looking at the sky*
*reflected! contemplating how the sun,*
*Great Rana, can thrust his yellow, webbed foot*
*through all the elements in a giant jump;*
*can poke the bottom of the brook; warm*
*the stumps for us to sit upon; and heat*
*our backs. Men have forgotten how to relax.*
*They bring their noisy boxes, and the blare*
*insults the air. We cannot hear the cheer*
*of crickets, nor our own dear booming chugs.*
*Frogs wouldn't ever eat men's legs.*
*We scorn their warm, dry princesses. We're proud*
*of our own bug-eyed brides with bouncing strides.*
*Keep your magic. We are not such fools.*
*Here is the ball without a claim on it.*
*We may begin from the same tadpoles, but*
*we've thought a bit, and will not turn to men.*

Here, too, the humblest creatures voice their opinions in a combination of sound ("We cannot hear the cheer / of crickets, nor our own dear booming chugs.") and symbol ("Frogs wouldn't ever eat men's legs.").

For some reason, frogs and toads seem to rivet (gribbet? grabbit?) the attention of children's book writers, and not just in poetry. There's Toad of *The Wind in the Willows*, the eternal toad of *Tuck Everlasting*, the friends in Lobel's Frog and Toad series,

Warton and Morton in *A Toad for Tuesday,* and "The Frog King" who retrieves the princess's golden ball in the German fairy tale. There is an endless parade of frogs and toads in folklore, not to mention mice and rabbits.

It must be an identification of children with small helpless animals that makes so many such creatures the center of poetry and folktales. In fact, Br'er Frog and Br'er Rabbit of the Uncle Remus stories leap to mind, as irresistible as their poetic counterparts.

Like poetry, a folktale catches fleeting feelings by the tail and holds them just long enough to enjoy. The two sure ways I have found to quiet down a car pool are chanting poetry and telling a story. In the early years, all I had to do was say "Boom, boom, we'll be there soon," which even the whiners thought hysterically funny at the age of two and a half. For my own sake I quickly increased my repertoire so that when the kids picked up and repeated the chant, which they invariably did, I could at least hear a varied replay. If chants cheered them up and diverted their attention from whacking each other over the head, a folktale or fairy tale really cast a spell of quiet attention over the whole group, broken only by an occasional screech over my driving as I got caught up in the story myself.

There is something breathtakingly clever about that helpless Br'er Rabbit fooling a tyrannical Bengal tiger into *begging* to have himself tied up to a tree. There's nothing like watching the little guy win, especially for a little child.

Such basic themes of the underdog—or underfrog,

as the case may be—defeating the overlord reverberate through collection after collection of folktales from every people and place. To count the themes of folklore is to count the heartbeat of the human race. It is said there are over 500 *known* versions of "Cinderella," which probably leaves a good many unknown. These are truly for an all-age audience. They've been told for centuries among mixed-generation groups of family and friends until hewn down to the common versions. When folklorists started to write them down in the 1700s and 1800s, the stories were frozen into print just the way children playing "Red Light, Green Light" are frozen into positions at the call of "Stop!"

Now we have selections, collections, translations, and illustrations to suit every whim, every shade of skin or experience. Just identify your family tree, go to the library, and dig into some of those roots.

In the Americana collections, there are tall tales from the West, Jack tales from the Southeast, Indian tales from every tribe in the country. Virginia Haviland's *North American Legends* and Alvin Schwartz's *Cross Your Fingers, Spit in Your Hat* are a good place to start, but there is really a rainbow of choices. *Womenfolk and Fairy Tales*, centered on heroic women, is only one of many working angles on collecting, and pioneer American only one of many traditions. The listing at the end of the chapter will speak for itself.

Folktales have inspired the same kind of endless listening that poetry has and the same kind of graphic re-creation, from contemporary artists such as Maurice

Sendak and Michael Foreman, who both illustrated fine editions of the Grimm tales, back to the earliest woodcuts for Gutenberg's first book of fables.

Folktales are time frozen, the epitome of ageless literature. Created, told, and retold to mixed groups of children and adults, they still wear well on every level. They are the bare bones of story. Each archetypal character represents a part of humanity, each action a part of life, each setting a part of existence. When the word "forest" appears, everyone understands it as a symbolic setting for losing the way, for dangers and confusion, for alienation from security and loved ones. Wolves, giants, kings, woodcutters, fools, beauties, all have distinctly defined roles. That's the secret of folktales' effective functioning in such a short space—they allow each person to imagine the kind of details that modern short stories and fiction must build into the narrative to be believable.

Any effort to clutter up an honorable old tale with irrelevant details is going to be a disaster. The language patterns are all set. They are not just part of the charm, but the very essence of the tale. To say that "the wedding party made merry through the night" represents wine, roasted suckling pig stuffed with apples, dancing, dogs cracking bones between their teeth, flirtatious pinches between serving men and scullery maids, singing of tales with a harp. "Made merry through the night" is a symbolic phrase that allows everyone to play the scene to their heart's content. To say that "the wedding party downed a couple of six-packs, grilled a steak, and joked around till

1:00 A.M." sounds likely but loses a lot of dignity, time-lessness, and space in which to elaborate. It narrows down the potential of the tale.

Calling a villain Grumble Bear is a lot less awe-some than calling it Growler. The first is a toy, the second an adversary. These are important points be-cause the language of folklore is the cue to the quality of the book you are getting. The telling of the tale can either kill it or make it live forever. Here are two passages from children's books describing the feats of tall tale heroes, the first a dull Bowleg Bill, the second a lively Finn McCool:

> Bowleg Bill, the cowboy, was in a rodeo. He threw two steers at the same time and won the bull-dogging contest. He lassoed a fly off a steer's back and won the roping contest. He won the rough-riding contest with a bucket of water balanced on his head. He didn't even spill a drop.

> Finn McCool was a giant but much too small for the work; the runt of the litter he was, yards shorter than his brothers and sisters, which was embarrassing. In fact, it is a better thing alto-gether to be a large dwarf than a small giant. Such a thing has been known to spoil a man's disposition entirely.

The first passage from Wyatt Blassingame's *Bowleg Bill: Seagoing Cowboy* has lost the music of words blended together and has been chopped into boring phrases. The second from Bernard Evslin's *The Green Hero: Early Adventures of Finn McCool* has kept the music and a good deal of the humor along with it. It's important to read a bit from any collection before you decide to take it home and live with it. A folktale or fairy tale does not have to be watered down for children, either in language or in content. Instead, it needs to be preserved with its original power and rolled off the tongue aloud, perhaps graced with some strong illustration, but never cutened up.

Folktales are every child's rich heritage. They go too deep to get a cheap surface treatment. In the right form they will reach you just as surely as they reach the child because, like poetry, they say so much in so few words that they are easy to carry in the mind. And whether you're old or young, it's important to visit places, occasionally, where real terrors lurk but true hearts live happily ever after.

## CHAPTER 7

### *Poems on the Move*

LARRICK, NANCY, editor. *Piping Down the Valleys Wild* (8 & up). Delacorte (hardcover); Dell Yearling (paper).
This unique collection ranges across old folk songs, poems from the Old Testament, classical and modern poets.

McCORD, DAVID. *One at a Time* (9 & up). Little, Brown.

A captivating collection of poems that reflects both
serious thought and gentle humor.

NESS, EVALINE. *Amelia Mixed the Mustard and Other
Poems* (6–12). Scribner's.

The focus is on girls in this engaging collection,
which combines good fun and first-rate poetry.

O'NEILL, MARY. *Hailstones and Halibut Bones* (6–12).
Doubleday (hardcover and paper).

Colors take on a new brilliance through images in
this kaleidoscope of poems.

*Oxford Book of Poetry for Children*, edited by Edward
Blishen (5–8). Watts.

A superb compendium of brilliantly illustrated
poems that appeal to children of all ages.

PRELUTSKY, JACK. *Nightmares: Poems to Trouble Your
Sleep* (8 & up). Greenwillow.

From witches to wizards, not to mention a bogey-
man or two, these ghostly verses send delightful
shivers up the spine.

SILVERSTEIN, SHEL. *Where the Sidewalk Ends* (5–8).
Harper & Row.

Breezy, humorous, and sensitive poems explore
the joys and fears of childhood with lively drawings that animate the text.

WILNER, ISABEL. *The Poetry Troupe* (8–13). Scribner's.

An exciting, well-rounded collection that reflects
children's interests; perfect for sharing and reading aloud.

WORTH, VALERIE. *More Small Poems* (9 & up). Farrar,
Straus & Giroux.

Small, everyday things are seen to be important
and valuable in these simple, inspiring poems.

## Tales That Move

ANDERSEN, HANS CHRISTIAN. *Dulac's The Snow Queen and Other Stories* (6–12). Doubleday.
Magnificent full-color plates enhance the magic of five of Andersen's best-loved stories.

FAULKNER, WILLIAM JAY. *The Days When the Animals Talked* (11 & up). Follett.
Robust tales of pride, strength, and courage celebrate the black folklore tradition.

THE BROTHERS GRIMM. *The Juniper Tree*, illustrated by Maurice Sendak (9 & up). Farrar, Straus & Giroux (hardcover); Dell Yearling (paper).
Enduring, classic tales of good and evil, illustrated by a master.

LANG, ANDREW. *The Blue Fairy Book* (6–12). Viking (hardcover); Dover (paper).
From all over the world, a collection of captivating tales that beg to be read aloud. This is one of the many "color" fairytale collections by Lang.

MINARD, ROSEMARY. *Womenfolk and Fairy Tales* (7–11). Houghton Mifflin.
Hale and hearty heroines take center stage in this collection of folklore.

RACKHAM, ARTHUR. *The Arthur Rackham Fairy Book* (9–12). Lippincott.
Superb illustrations highlight this collection of traditional tales.

ROCKWELL, ANNE. *The Three Bears and Fifteen Other Stories* (5–10). Crowell.
Sixteen favorite stories, from the Gingerbread Man to the Three Billy Goats Gruff, are told with verve, gusto, and humor.

SINGER, ISAAC BASHEVIS. *Zlateh the Goat and Other Stories* (6–12). Harper & Row (hardcover and paper).
Seven engaging stories from middle-European Jewish folklore, retold in a lively spirit by the Nobel Prize-winning author.

## *True or False?*
## *Factual Books for Children*

# 8

I was pushing a stroller along once when suddenly a series of excited noises came out of it. They sounded something like "Oh Dee Dee Dee Dee Dee Dee Dee!" A pudgy finger shot out from under the fringed awning and waved frantically toward the sky. All I could see was an airplane.

That's the big difference between the first airplane and the thousandth, that rush of excitement. For anyone who has forgotten the wonder of watching an airplane fly overhead, or a rainstorm come up, or the curiosity of how airplanes, thunder, and lightning are made, there's something refreshing about being with kids who haven't. It restores your sense of balance in varying degrees, depending on how lopsided that has become and how fresh the child's view is.

Because there is so much that children don't know, facts are as miraculous as fiction for them. Everyone knows the question-and-answer stage. "Where do I come from? What makes the stars white? Why do dogs pee on the tree?" Most adults are stumped by such queries. Even those who keep calm and look things up in the encyclopedia together with a child will never get to the end of the cross-examination.

As bothersome as this stage may seem, it is the sign of an explosively growing mind. In the matter of education, a child's own curiosity is the greatest tool. It starts long before school does and is a driving force in growing up. And it can be a joy to jaded adults.

Perhaps my favorite sign, next to Big Tomato and the park bathroom poem, is the one over the entrance to the Smithsonian Institute, "Knowledge begins in wonder." It does. Educational systems that dampen wonder are taking a chance with passing on knowledge. The habit of finding things out independently can start with the habit of looking through books at a preschool age. Nonfiction for children has mushroomed in quantity and quality to titles on every conceivable subject, from words to World War II.

Whatever the child of your choice is interested in, there is bound to be a book or many on the subject. This will probably require a trip to the local public or school library. Some bookstores stock informational books for children, but if you can't find what you want, just order it.

Good juvenile nonfiction serves up information straight from the hip, without any patronizing remarks to try to sweeten up natural phenomena that are dynamic to begin with. The format will be clean, the illustrations both clear and interesting. The information will be current, well-organized, accurate, lucid, and presented with enthusiasm and cited sources of authority. If this sounds familiar, it is exactly the same set of criteria you look for in an adult book of information.

In addition, the extra dash of skill required for fiction goes for nonfiction too: it must be carved down to basics without distortion or oversimplification. The word "stomach," for instance, should never be substituted for the accurate term "womb" in a discussion of reproduction, because to do so would generate multiple misconceptions. Children should learn the right word rather than vaguely associate pregnancy with eating. On the other hand, they don't need to know yet the complications of breech birth or multiple conception.

What, for instance, is a child supposed to make of the statement that Daddy plants a seed in Mommy? Or to move from biology to history, that Abraham Lincoln was killed while sitting in a box? Or that "All his life, Prince Charles has been learning how to do things"? These statements have all appeared in juvenile science books or biographies, along with misleading illustrations. One introduction to the human body showed a diagram of huge black sperm without any caption or indication of the actual microscopic size. No wonder kids grow up with fuzzy ideas.

Fictionalizing facts is another offender in books of information. Earl the Squirrel's marriage to Mrs. Squirrel, pictured with wedding ring, is not the best

introduction to animal habits. Animals that think
and feel like people are all right in fantasy, but they
violate the truth of science, which is exciting in its
own right. So is the truth of history. Nobody needs
distortions like the portrayal of the great English
social reformer Elizabeth Fry as a child talking with
a butterfly: " 'Why are you so sad, pretty lady?' . . . 'I
am sad because I am not being kind enough to people.' " Nor of the cutesy cartoon accompanying that
statement. Nor, for that matter, does anyone need
recipes that forget to tell youngsters to cook the
chicken before cutting it up and putting it in the
salad. Nor of prehistoric mammals with blood spill-
ing luridly from their fangs as they haul away a cave
woman. The natural and man-made world is an in-
finitely exciting place without being artificially and
dishonestly spiced up, covered up, or served up.

If a text raises questions in your own mind with
doubtful statements ("Children who go to museums
and read dinosaur books love dinosaurs. But most
scientists don't. . . ."); if a text makes you jump back
and forth and never get things quite straightened
out; if its explanations lead you back again and again
to reread; if it does not cite sources, or cites statistics
that are outdated; if the author has written books
about anything and everything rather than focusing
on a deeply developed field of interest; if he or she
skims the surface of fact without delving into what it
means; if the information is dumped on the reader
in a dull or jumbled heap—you have every reason to
question this as a valid and valuable book for children, whether you are an expert in the given subject

or have never heard of it. Those are a lot of "ifs," but the material included in and left out of a book, the skill of presentation, the writing and format, are all as important as the information itself.

Not that long ago, for instance, American children learned American history minus black people. There simply was little or no mention of their hard-fought rise in our society from enslaved possessions to free and influential citizens. Before many textbooks began to make tentative revisions including occasional black leaders and their contributions, Julius Lester wrote *To Be a Slave*. It shares with *Never to Forget: The Jews of the Holocaust* an historical honesty grounded in firsthand sources and carefully researched facts, all presented from the point of view of an objective but deeply involved writer. Both authors have brought facts to life in the shape of people, to be introduced as "living" information. Both write to be read and experienced, not just to be mentally stuffed away in a file of factual feedback.

Not all children's nonfiction is so serious. History itself abounds with the humor that is inevitable where human beings are the subject. Jean Fritz's series on American leaders such as George Washington, Paul Revere, and John Hancock show their foibles as well as their strengths, a refreshing balance after the kind of adulatory biographies that used to lead children (many of whom maintained such illusions into adulthood) to believe that political figures were the image of perfection.

With similar gentle irreverence, Barbara Seuling's *You Can't Eat Peanuts in Church and Other Little-*

*Known Laws* shows some of the oddities that are part of our legal works:

> In Idaho, you cannot fish for trout from the back of a giraffe.

> In San Francisco, you are forbidden by law to spit on your laundry.

> Lions are not permitted to run wild on the streets of Alderson, West Virginia.

> In Baltimore, Maryland, it is against the law to mistreat an oyster.

> An animal on the street after dark in Berea, Ohio, must display a red tail light.

> In Michigan you may not hitch a crocodile to a fire hydrant.

> It is unlawful for goldfish to ride on a Seattle, Washington, bus unless they lie still.

There's nothing funnier than actual facts. Ferdinand Monjo has written a string of witty perspectives on historical characters, from Mozart (*Letters to Horseface*) to Benjamin Franklin (*Poor Richard in France*), weaving facts into stories. These carry on an early tradition of entertaining historical fiction for children, two of the early favorites being the humorous *Ben and Me* and *Mr. Revere and I* by Robert Lawson, along with the gripping *Johnny Tremain* by Esther Forbes. All of these cross over from history to fiction but still give the full flavor and facts of the times as a result of the authors' careful research.

Because of the vivid paintings illustrating it, Joe Lasker's *Merry Ever After* was something of a landmark history when it came out in 1976. The book contrasted two weddings that might have taken place in the Middle Ages, one between nobility, one between peasants. Pleasing to look at, it did not spare some of the hard facts of medieval life.

In presenting information graphically, children's science books have become a showcase for photography. One of the outstanding examples of information combined in text and photographs is Patricia Lauber's *What's Hatching Out of That Egg?* In addition to an uncommonly interesting array of hatching creatures that keep the reader guessing what comes next is a wide scope of facts that readers will answer for themselves—one of the principles of scientific inquiry.

Lennart Nilsson, a famous Swedish photographer, used his innovative technique for photographing live fetuses in utero to illustrate a children's book on reproduction, *How Was I Born?* Although it was not as well-organized or well-written as a number of other titles on sex and reproduction (several good ones are recommended in the list following this chapter), and although it is more frankly revealing than some parents can handle (notice I didn't say "children"), the color photographs are a fine introduction to the whole process of procreation. Parents who hesitate to plunge into the facts of life with their children through books may find themselves a lot more uncomfortable later on with the results of other ways their children learn the lay of the land. There are certainly plenty of children's books today to do the job at all levels of understanding and modesty.

People who feel more at home with other aspects of the birds and bees will find them well covered too. Any of Millicent Selsam's scientific presentations on plants and animals, especially those photographed by Jerome Wexler, can turn the next walk into an exploration of nature. Their *Maple Tree* marked the first time I had ever really understood the reproduction of plants, even though I had memorized the descriptions offered in the same biology course as the dead frogs. Two favorite titles with children are *Peanut* and *Popcorn*, which show the beauty and practical efficiency of nature in action on one of her most common products. Two other books that fascinate all ages are Nina Leen's photo essays on bats and snakes, while Ozzie Sweet and Jack Scott have introduced on camera a whole series of animals from buffalo to prairie dogs.

Good photography is not confined to science books. Children and adults alike are drawn to Jill Krementz's series, *A Very Young Dancer, A Very Young Rider, A Very Young Gymnast,* and *A Very Young Skater.* Each shows the glamour and drudgery of areas many children dream of entering, and at a very young age. They show a world of work where commitment knows no age limits, where children and adults are not separated along artificial lines. The common denominator is talent. Young readers are drawn by their peers' ambitions being taken seriously and realized successfully, while older readers find the rigorous training of such star performers fascinating.

On the other end of the line from Krementz's world of career prodigies is the equally popular hobby book that answers that old familiar whine of "I'm bored" on a rainy day. Steven Caney's *Kids' America* is a handy kind of answer. It will consume hours of attention, of making, doing, playing, and finding out. You can either grab it and give it to the whiner for some peace and quiet or join in the fun yourself. It is the ultimately practical craft/whole earth catalogue for all ages.

Over the years the market has been deluged with more specialized titles on everything from carving pumpkins to cutting out puppets. Note well, those elders who find themselves secretly drawn toward the model plane, train, and car counters: the craft shelves are a hobbyist's field day. Children have the good sense not to be embarrassed by such interests. Take advantage of the situation and exploit it for your own indulgence. Two of my middle-aged friends spend their weekends on their knees, running model trains —and they don't even have children. But they do have the latest children's books on model trains.

If you get hold of the right book, you may even learn how to beat your kid at chess. In art, crafts, and cooking, children's books can be a real blessing. Your heart sinks as you hear you're supposed to produce your child's class play costume—a pterodactyl? Go to the library. If there's not a children's book on how to make pterodactyl costumes (and there may be one by now), at least there will be books with clear illustrations of pterodactyls and books with ingenious tips on creating crazy costumes that will turn out okay in spite of the most uncoordinated pair of hands.

Before I got hold of a good basic juvenile (i.e., clear and simple) introduction to knitting, my practice sweaters looked like they might fit a boa constrictor. Jessie Rubenstone's *Knitting for Beginners* changed all that.

Whatever your craft problem, it can be solved by the kind of illustrated, step-by-step approach used in a well-planned children's book. You can pick up a new skill yourself at the same time the child is learning how to do it. Making mistakes together is more fun than making them alone.

Sports biographies, manuals on gymnastic techniques, baseball, and horseback riding are all available for the asking. Riddle books are rampant. These go over well during that age when the entire conversation seems to consist of fourth-grade jokes. Jane Sarnoff and Reynold Ruffins's *What? A Riddle Book* is one of the wackiest contributions. In fact, whether they're spotlighting riddles, bicycles, chess, aquariums, or space, this team makes every subject easy on the eyes. Their pop art and nicely designed graphic formats set an intriguing new standard for humorous items that are often just slapped into book form any old way.

One of the best pieces of children's nonfiction that has been published is an introduction to bookmaking itself. It was put out by a juvenile department, but I often see Howard Greenfeld's *Books: From Writer to*

*Reader* placed in the adult section of bookstores. I'm glad adults are enjoying it for themselves; still, I always sneak a few copies back into the juvenile shelf so they'll pick it up for children as well.

There is plenty for children to learn and there are plenty of books they can learn from. It is surprising how many tidbits an adult can pick up with them along the way. It's always a jolt to realize how much we adults have closed off to the kind of ongoing exploration kids come by naturally.

For an introduction to an unknown subject— worms, wizards, willow trees, or electric motors—you couldn't do better than a good children's book. Next time those nagging questions start up, join in the search for an answer. The process may start with a book and lead to a new awareness, and for the child, a lifelong habit of thought.

## CHAPTER 8

### *Getting the Facts*

BEWLEY, SHEILA, and MARGARET SHEFFIELD. *Where Do Babies Come From?* (5–8). Knopf.
A gentle explanation, accompanied by moving artwork, of human conception and childbirth.
CANEY, STEVEN. *Steven Caney's Kids' America* (8 & up). Workman.
A whole earth catalogue of things to make and do with children.

COLE, JOANNE. *A Chick Hatches* (5–8). Morrow. Close-up photographs detail the wonder and drama of a chick growing in its egg.

COMFORT, ALEX and JANE. *The Facts of Love: Living, Loving, and Growing Up* (11 & up). Crown.
A natural, open look at sex features accurate, complete, well-organized information and frank pictures.

FRITZ, JEAN. *And Then What Happened, Paul Revere?* (8 & up). Coward McCann.
An exciting, funny version of Paul Revere's famous ride.

GRILLONE, LISA and JOSEPH GENNARO. *Small Worlds Close Up* (8 & up). Crown.
Microphotography gives a beautiful new perspective on ordinary objects.

KREMENTZ, JILL. *A Very Young Gymnast* (8 & up). Knopf.
Color photos and text convey the joy, pain, and triumph of a young girl's gymnastic training.

LESHAN, EDA. *What's Going to Happen to Me? When Parents Separate or Divorce* (8 & up). Scribner's (hardcover); School Book Service (paper).
Sensible, supportive advice to help children cope in a family crisis.

LESTER, JULIUS. *To Be a Slave* (12 & up). Dial (hardcover); Dell Laurel-Leaf (paper).
A powerful chronicle of tragedy skillfully assembled from the eloquent slaves themselves.

MELTZER, MILTON. *Never to Forget: The Jews of the Holocaust* (12 & up). Harper & Row (hardcover); Dell Laurel-Leaf (paper).

The horrors of Nazi Germany are vividly presented in this moving account of the Holocaust.

PRINGLE, LAURENCE. *Death Is Natural* (6–11). School Book Service.

Death is explained in a simple, reassuring way as a part of the natural process of life.

MAURICE SENDAK

## The Goose Is Loose—
### Sex, Violence, Obscenity, Tragedy,
### Scariness, Life, and Other Controversies

# 9

We want the best of all possible worlds for our children. That's understandable, but it surely demands an impossible idealism from their books. It amounts to asking that children hear no evil, see no evil, speak no evil, taste no evil. Yet those requirements contradict the very existence of literature, because literature is a mirror of the world. Children know there is evil as well as good in the world. The trick is to learn to cope with it. To do that, a child needs to learn how to recognize it, how to sort it out.

One of the complicating factors is that everyone defines evil in a different way. Is it sex, obscenity, violence, simplistic politics, heretical religion, bad writing, clumsy art, or taking a bite out of your friend? And who's to say for children, other than your own? In fact, who's to say for them? They are separate human beings who will make their own choices, inasmuch as they are allowed to grow up. As parents, we may not always like our children's choices, but ultimately they will make them, one way or another, when they establish their independence.

That can be a rude surprise, but there's a way to prepare for it. We can't keep children from thinking and wouldn't want to. What we *can* do is take a position of leadership in their thought by opening up issues and discussing them. It's a lot more effective to join in reading what children are reading and to express reasoned opinions of it than to hide or confiscate a book. Partners can discuss books; it's dictators who have to forbid them. And partnership breeds respect, while dictatorship breeds rebellion. It's not just theoretical rights of the child at stake in an open-book policy, it's what works best.

There is an inordinate attraction to things forbidden. For every book taken off the shelf by a blue-ribbon committee objecting to some sinful passage in it, five avid readers of it rise from the ranks. Remember hiding whatever book, magazine, or comic it was you hid under your mattress? Anyone's natural curiosity is aroused by having to peek into the keyhole and pry open the lock instead of walking right through the open door. Then, of course, curiosity is blissfully satisfied by discovering that the forbidden book deals exactly with what is most interesting, from sex to social problems.

Here's a typical letter of objection to a junior novel,

Norma Fox Mazer's *Saturday, The Twelfth of October,* and my (equally) typical reply:

"Your review does not mention that one of the main themes was the symbolic use of a lack of menstruating as a dominant fear of a girl. If you know seventh and eighth graders you will know what a carnival they would have with this. Ours are no different than other junior high people, I'm sure, and anything dealing with a sexual theme or profanity is grist for their mill. Because of this, even though I found it a well-developed novel, I did not feel that I could put it on our shelves."

Reply: "Menstruation should not be signaled or warned against or classified with profanity. It should be included in junior high students' books exactly because it *is* 'grist for their mill'—in other words, of significant and natural interest to them in their stage of development. As long as it is treated with dignity and ease, as it is here, I would hate to think that a descriptive plot summary would keep librarians from ordering it. You yourself found it a well-developed novel and did not mention exactly why the symbol of menstruation was in poor taste; it seems to me that young people's dominant fears should be discussed in their literature."

There was an outcry over fourteen swear words in Johanna Reiss's novel, *The Upstairs Room,* which dealt with the hardships visited on two children by Hitler's drive to exterminate the Jews during World War II. People did a lot worse than swear on the Western Front, but, to be true to the situation, they *did* occasionally swear. To re-create the reality of some characters, scenes, and settings, literature must include profanity or street language; this is nothing young readers don't know and can't keep in context. Those fourteen damns that somebody took the trouble to count seem pretty mild in light of the traumatic experiences and burning issues of war, as portrayed in a well-written, realistic but not violent novel about an unavoidable past.

There is certainly a valid place for concern about the horrors to which children can be exposed, but many controversies seem to have nothing to do with the real horrors. Most objections center around occasional profanity or mild sexuality, which are regular parts of a child's real world. The question is, should we lie and say they don't exist or teach children how to deal with them?

Hardly a week goes by without a children's or young adult book being banned from the shelves somewhere. Every once in a while a particularly volatile situation makes the news. But the books that elicit concern rarely involve real violence to the human spirit or body. The throwing overboard of babies from a slave ship, the brutal killing of a gang member, the abuse of a child have all appeared in children's books without causing a ripple of objection. It seems to be the puritanical taboos of our society that raise eyebrows, not the harm that may be done to children's psyches. It's what we ourselves have trouble dealing with, not what *children* have trouble dealing with. Because times are changing so fast, it's not easy to stay in touch with children whose world differs so much from our

own childhoods of the past. Some pressures and problems will always remain the same, but others are pro-
foundly new and different.

Because of this, writers and publishers are now taking greater moral risks with more children's books
than ever before. They are dealing with more problems of significance in our society, and they are head-
ing further and further into controversy. It has become
almost a platitude that children's books these days are
a controversial item, with frankness in language and
subject that was never dreamed of years ago and that
raises more and more hackles as time goes on.

"Sweetness and light" is an order long past in children's literature. It never was a reality in most children's lives. Today, children are confronted both in
the media and in their everyday reality with situations
involving drug addiction, alcoholism, irresponsible
sex, extramarital pregnancy, abortion, child abuse,
rape, insanity, murder, suicide, prostitution, gang violence, death (by war, accident, and disease), personal
conflicts ranging from divorce to homosexual relation-
ships, handicaps, senility, poverty, abandonment, and
racism, together with all the sociopolitical isms that
abound . . . trouble never comes in ones. Sometimes
several of the above crowd into a single life, and so
into a single story.

That is not so much a conscious decision on the
writer's part as a reflection through the writer of what
our society is, of what we are all going through.
Writers and artists of integrity shouldn't be attacked
for artistic honesty about what is going on around
them, nor children for their need to know and under-

stand. A troubled society provokes troubling books. As one character says to his readers in Paul Zindel's *Confessions of a Teenage Baboon*:

> The last thing I've got to tell you is there are things that are done to me in this story that aren't very nice—but I'm going to tell you anyway because maybe some of you will learn something from them. Maybe there are some of you who are as ashamed and mixed up as I was and don't know how to handle the problems of being alive that people don't warn you about. And that's the main reason I'm writing this confession—because I don't think we should go on keeping quiet about these things. All the lying has to stop somewhere. The only thing that's going on in my mind is that I hope when you finish reading this you won't hate me. Please don't despise me for being the one to tell you that the days of being Huckleberry Finn are gone forever.

The important thing to remember in sorting out thoughts about literature that deals with untraditional or sensational themes is not to view the books in isolation. These books reflect basic changes in our times. Books for children have always been a mirror of society's threats as well as its ideals. Early children's books were haunted by the fire and brimstone of hell, along with the religious rewards or punishments of those who had or had not sinned. In their own tortured way, those books were every bit as shocking as the sex and obscenity that outrages some parents today. It is not the authors who are to blame, or the publishers, but our own society. Most writers are simply being honest about what they see, and most children, just like adults, would prefer not to be lied to.

Some controversial books are for the young or middle-grade readers, but most fall into the category of teen-age or young adult novel. They are published out of the juvenile trade departments, with an eye toward occasional adult readers through paperback reprint sales. Sometimes the line between juvenile and adult becomes fuzzy. Fran Arrick's *Steffie Can't Come Out to Play*, for instance, is the first-person narrative of an unhappy fourteen-year-old who dreams of glamour and recognition. She runs away from her small town and becomes a prostitute in the streets of New York City to survive when she finds she can't fulfill her dreams.

It may sound unusual for a children's book, but it's not all that unusual among our children, as statistics on runaway adolescents show. In fact, because the book is for an adolescent audience, the author has treated the plot with a good deal more care and dignity than one might imagine possible, given the potential for sensational details. The situations ring true, the characterizations are drawn with care, the scenes are sensitively controlled. The book is indisputably a moral tale.

On what grounds, then, does anyone ban the book? It's certainly not an *advertisement* for the bad life. If anything, it's a case study, a *warning* that this is something that can (and does) happen to unsuspecting kids. At the very least, the reader will conclude that problems are best worked out on the home front. Steffie is lucky. With some outside intervention, she extricates herself from a typically complicated relationship with her pimp and gets back home. Many kids know this goes on. Should they pretend not to? It may have happened in their family or to a friend or some acquaintance in school. Is it enough to know and look away?

There are just no easy answers in reacting to books like this. In the old days those would have sounded like soap operas. Now they sound like the six o'clock news.

Books for younger ages reflect the same kinds of trouble. In one year there were nine novels for grade school readers involving child abuse. One story had a young girl used as a police lure for a psychotic rapist/killer, while in another a girl was almost killed by her insane mother. A fantasy called *The Borribles* set a record for violent deaths and cynical endings. A historical novel included a sexual scene between mother and son. A southern period piece had an unbalanced preacher assaulting a child. A picture book portrayed a princess whose beauty instantly blinded those who looked upon her—and she would accept no less as a token of true love. The story ended with the drowning of both the princess and the only one who loved her enough to look and go blind.

Of course, none of the books mentioned have been presented in terms other than plot. There's been no examination of quality, which is the important guideline discussed in Chapter 6. Some had moving characters and skillful writing, others cardboard characters and pedestrian writing; some had a dynamic effect, others a contrived structure. On the whole, realistic "problem novels" form only a small part of the market. Nobody would read them back to back except a reviewer who had no choice. But when people say "trends" in children's books, this is often the kind of book they are talking about—the kind that attracts a brief notice in national and local newspapers as being banned from the library shelf because of content. When they ask "what's going on," they mean "what's going on way out front that might cause trouble?"

It may be some comfort to find out from reviewers of adult literature that books in that area—and not just the new ones—are a lot more vulgar. Once, when I was interviewed on television, an irate viewer called in and chastised me for recommending *any* of these newfangled books for children. Children, he said, ought to be reading the Bible. I agreed with him that children ought to be reading the Bible—it's a profound work—but it's got stories in it that are a lot wilder than anything I've seen in a children's book. Those times were grim, too, and it showed up just as clearly in the literature.

The fact is, kids need some well-written books about what's going on in their world; otherwise literature will seem at best irrelevant and at worst hypocritical. Fantasy and science fiction can offer popular escape routes into other worlds, but realistic fiction must travel this one as honestly as possible. Even fantasy and science fiction must, as Jillsy Sloper said in *The World According to Garp*, "feel true." And kids do want to read these books, just as they read *Jaws* and *The Godfather* in the recent past, *Forever Amber* and *From Here to Eternity* thirty years ago, and many other "questionable" selections from the adult best seller list.

There may be one gratifying difference, one element that worried or outraged adults should take into consideration before censoring controversial children's books. While skill obviously varies, it is rare to find a writer in the world of juvenile literature who does not care deeply about childhood, the pain and pleasure of growing up, about children—and who does not shape the resulting material with that care.

When factual books are banned from the open shelves, they are often the very kinds of facts children need most, on reproduction and birth control, for instance. And there are still parts of the country where children cannot find out about evolution or Communism from a school or library book on that subject. In each case, the information is considered a threat and so kept hidden away.

The ironic thing is that some of the most liberal organizations in the country have spearheaded the most conservative tactics in banning anything considered politically or socially unacceptable. The picture of a black woman shown doing the dishes has been decried as racist and sexist—double whammy— no matter what the context. An old man pictured in a rocking chair has been absurdly interpreted as being in an "ageist" position because such a posture shows no respect for people over sixty-five.

All kinds of ideas and ideals are imposed as stand-

ards on children's books in a way they never are on
adult books because children are seen as impression-
able, to be molded in the right form. The sacrifice of
truth is often made in books for children which reflect
real life—in the attempt to control the message for the
child.

The question of how to protect our children from
harm is an important one. They start out so small,
defenseless, and trusting that we never want a blow to
fall. In order to protect them, we control them. But
control and protection are two different things. It's
important to *keep* the love part of the control and
*keep out* the fear and insecurity that lead to over-
control, or a wish to force children into thinking the
way we want them to. That amounts to power, not
protection. Sometimes it's hard to sort out the two.

Being permissive is certainly not the answer. Per-
missiveness doesn't work any better than force, because children need direction and want limits to keep
themselves safe. The key seems to be a realistic, responsible involvement in a child's knowledge and
activities. It takes time and energy, and books make
one of the best meeting grounds for an exchange of
opinion. No one can deny feelings and physiology in
the long run; they'll come out one way or the other.
It's best for adult and child to pull up the shades
together and take a good look at what's going on.

There is no question, for instance, that today's
teenagers are going to have sex education. But is it
going to be from the media, from peers, or from a
responsible adult? There is no question that they will
eventually experience sex, one way or another. Again,

it is a question of when and how. The more they've had time to think and talk about sex in the sheltered and loving environment of their homes, the better prepared they will be to make choices and not be victims of circumstance, as in the case of so many pregnant teenagers who have been caught by surprise. Most adults want children eventually to find sex comfortable, not guilty or furtive or destructive. The right attitude can be formulated a lot better over a book than in the back seat of a car.

Reading, in fact, can be the least harmful first encounter with the controversial problems. Of course, powerful writing can twist anyone's dreams into nightmares; even cheap pulp can have unpredictable effects. But both of these are one step removed from experience and give the inexperienced scope for thinking without having to react.

Sometimes what captures public indignation is funny, especially in picture books. People have objected to Raymond Briggs's *Father Christmas* because Santa enjoys a sip of cognac thoughtfully left for him by an understanding father and at another point squats comfortably on the toilet. John Steptoe's *My Special Best Words* also drew some fire because it shows a child sitting on the toilet. Many small children, after all, spend a good deal of their time on the toilet just learning how to use it. Surely it doesn't hurt them to see somebody else achieving success.

It's hard to predict what will provoke criticism. Margaret Mahy's *The Boy Who Was Followed Home* raised alarm because the boy got rid of the hippopotami by swallowing a pill; *Mr. and Mrs. Pig's Eve-*

*ning Out,* because the baby-sitter was a wolf; *Some Swell Pup,* because Maurice Sendak's pictures illustrate a dog peeing; *Wind Rose* by Crescent Dragonwagon, because it shows a child's parents discreetly wrapped up in a blanket together in bed; *The Bear and the Fly* by Paula Winter, because so much furniture is destroyed in the bear's chasing the fly; *Ben's Trumpet* by Rachel Isadora, because a boy's father is shown elbow-deep in a poker game; and *Rapunzel,* because, in an old version, the long-haired heroine has twins before she and the prince have a chance to marry and live happily ever after. The most alarming thing about any of these picture books, really, would be a child's missing out on them.

Ironically, the same people who object to books may allow television to baby-sit their children for hours every day; and television, while more graphically detailed, does not allow the same scope for thinking. Whereas the ability to read a book guarantees certain levels of intellectual development, television can barrage the brain of the youngest child via visual and aural reception. This child may be unprepared intellectually, emotionally, and experientially.

Thinking involves getting a message, processing it, and reacting to it. Watching television all day long can slow down intellectual development by curtailing a critical thought process. If children can learn to respond to television, it can be used constructively, but they must learn to act as critics, not gullible receptacles of the message delivered. Their reading, on the other hand, both depends on and furthers a more individually varied, active, and deeper range of experience. Reading is a gentle but strong step toward knowledge for the unexposed child.

I mention television so you'll know I know it exists. There have been enough words written about TV and its effects on society to sink the *Titanic*. Television is constantly dragged into competition with books, but it doesn't really belong there. It's distracting to compare the two. Books and television (or movies) can and do stimulate each other, as we've seen with *Little House on the Prairie* or *Mary Poppins*. However, television must be watched selectively rather than continuously. Given the nature of most television programs today, a children's book is likely to be more stimulating to a child's independent thought and imagination.

For both media, it is important to ask the same questions. What's honest and what's exploitative? What's fad and what's for keeps? What's open-minded and what's mindless?

For me, violence is the thing that most often raises these questions. Obscenity seems harmless by comparison, and sex should not be lumped together with problems in the first place. But a book or program must be very moving and meaningful for me to feel it's worth a violent scene that will intrude on my mind and dreams. I feel the same way about my child's books or programs. As strongly as I react to violence as a violation, and as much as I would like to keep violence away from my child's sight and experience, I know I can't. Violence *is* part of her world. I hate it, I have trouble with it, I wish it would go away, but there it is. She sees and hears of rape, murder, and war almost every day through adult conversations, in newspapers, on television, or by rumor. These things have touched her life and may sometime invade it.

When I feel the impulse to keep her away from books that deal with violence, I have to tread carefully. We live in a violent world. She and I had better learn to deal with it now, while she has the security of my home and the benefit of my experience. We can read and talk together about what's good, what's bad, what's upsetting, what's moving, what's cruel, what's worthwhile, what must be faced, what should be turned off or objected to.

I have to ask myself the questions all of us must answer individually regarding any troublesome element in a child's world. First, should such a problem appear at all in children's books? My conscience answers yes, because the problem exists and has to be prepared for. Second, how should it be treated if it does appear? My own standard demands a combination of skill, care, and imagination. Third, who decides what is a problem in the first place? I believe it must be the child and I, for ourselves only. And finally, who enforces that decision, and on whom? This, too, is between individual child and parent.

What I consider a problem may not violate someone else as much as other kinds of things might. I would hate to have a school principal decide a book must come off the shelf—out of my child's reach— because another child's parent demanded it removed; or out of another child's reach because I demanded it removed. No one should *have* to read a book but everyone should have the right to.

Censorship is a private decision. When it goes public, somebody's rights are going to get stepped on.

My own experience is that children don't need censorship; what they need is adult involvement. There is a big difference. It's easier to say "get rid of it" than to say "let's face it."

*Sam, Bangs, and Moonshine,* a picture book by Evaline Ness that won the Caldecott Medal in 1967, is the story of a young girl who can't tell the difference between a fantasy and a lie—she sends a playmate on a chase that almost kills him. Samantha finally learns that, although she needn't give up her dragons and magic carpets, she must perceive and communicate clearly what is real. We must learn the same thing. Giving children any less than our best perception of reality is a costly mistake.

## CHAPTER 9

### *Groundbreaking Books*

BLUME, JUDY. *Forever* (12 & up). Bradbury (hardcover); Pocket Books (paper).

For high school seniors Katherine and Michael, first love brings intense emotional and sexual responses.

CORMIER, ROBERT. *The Chocolate War* (12 & up). Pantheon (hardcover); Dell Laurel-Leaf (paper).

The one teenage boy who refuses to participate

in a high school fund-raising campaign faces terrifying consequences at the hands of the system.

DONOVAN, JOHN. *Wild in the World* (12 & up). Harper & Row (hardcover); Avon (paper).

When the last member of his family dies, young John seeks comfort and companionship from a half-wild wolf-dog in this moving portrayal of an extraordinary relationship.

HOLLAND, ISABELLE. *The Man Without a Face* (12 & up). Lippincott (hardcover); Dell Laurel-Leaf (paper).

Lonely fourteen-year-old Charles turns to his aloof tutor for friendship and learns that love can have many faces.

KERR, M. E. *Dinky Hocker Shoots Smack!* (12 & up). Harper & Row (hardcover); Dell Laurel-Leaf (paper).

Dinky's not a drug addict—she's a food addict. But a fat problem just isn't enough to attract her parents' attention.

KLEIN, NORMA. *Mom, the Wolfman, and Me* (10 & up). Pantheon (hardcover); Avon (paper).

Brett and her mom have a terrific relationship, but is there room in their unconventional lifestyle for a third party?

SENDAK, MAURICE. *In the Night Kitchen* (4–8). Harper & Row.

In an amazing dream, Mickey flies out of his clothes, into a cake, and through the air in a plane made of batter.

SPARKS, BEATRICE. *Go Ask Alice* (12 & up). Prentice-Hall (hardcover); Avon (paper).

A diary details the tragedy of a teen-age girl's introduction to the drug culture—and the horrors she finds there.

WEIK, MARY. *The Jazz Man* (8 & up). Atheneum.
A deserted child turns to music and memories for comfort.

ZINDEL, PAUL. *Pardon Me, You're Stepping on My Eyeball* (12 & up). Harper & Row (hardcover); Bantam (paper).
The offbeat story of two teen-agers—"Marsh" Mellow and Edna Shinglebox—who meet in group therapy and help each other out of their confusion.

GARTH WILLIAMS

## *The Treasure Hunt—How to Track Down Good Books*

# 10

Having a head full of ideas and titles can make the search for children's books challenging—or frustrating. The local bookstore may offer little more than a handful of Nancy Drew mysteries and a classic or two. The public library may be unfamiliar. Your children's classroom experience may be limited to textbooks and their school library nonexistent. It may be hard to select quality items from the selection of mass market (widely distributed) book products that *are* available in grocery and variety stores. And finally, there may arise differences of judgment between you and your child.

Such situations are typical, but don't give up. There's gold at the end of the rainbow. It's all in knowing how to find it. The key is persistence. One strike is worth a lot of digging.

The best place to start is the closest public library. Your tax dollars already support it, so you might as well take advantage of it. It's a gold mine of information, books, and other resources. The librarian will be familiar with some of the titles mentioned and will either have them on the shelves, get them from other libraries, or suggest similar titles that are available.

You may also discover free story hours, film programs, and book clubs at the library, all for the asking. On afternoons when everyone needs to get out and the park is cold or crowded or just visited once too often, try that library. You can stock up on adult books at the same time.

Libraries are often open evenings for working parents, who are least likely to have time to spend with their kids during the day. A bridge of books between parent and child is an ideal way to span the gap between their separate worlds. A weekly visit to the library can solidly structure a bridge that will survive various stages from childhood dependency through adolescent rebellion.

The American Library Association publishes a helpful list of Notable Children's Books every year. This list will either be available at local libraries or can be ordered directly from The American Library Association, 50 E. Huron, Chicago, Illinois 60611. Almost all libraries feature national and state award books. Again, just ask. Nobody becomes a children's librarian without a bit of missionary zeal to convert people into booklovers, and the bewildered adult is a prime candidate for conversion!

If you find yourself signing out the same books over and over, maybe they're worth owning. Prepare for a trip to the bookstore and *ask for it*. Books not in stock can easily be ordered. You may even want to pass on a list of books to the salesperson with a suggestion to stock up on a few for the other parents and children in the community.

If your budget is tight, have the salesperson check *Paperback Books in Print*, which may allow you to buy five books instead of one. Even picture books are beautifully reproduced in paperback these days and are surprisingly sturdy.

When bookstore owners sense a new interest in their clientele, they will often reevaluate their stock; it's worth establishing a personal relationship through visits and conversations with salespeople. Chain store dealers are less accessible, but they can afford to stock more, especially in the juvenile paperback department. *Encyclopedia Brown* by Donald Sobol is one of B. Dalton's juvenile best sellers and would be a sure-fire hit to start off your elementary reader's involvement.

Another trick to shopping for what's available is learning to spot quality even in supermarket racks, where distributors often pile up a lot of junk. There are good Golden Books and bad ones; there's interesting Disney and dull Disney; there are beautiful pop-up and other "gadget" books along with ugly, cluttered ones; there are funny comics and violent ones.

Make comparisons and trust your own taste. Look especially for clean artistic design, interesting writing, and a warm, ingenuous quality *in any book anywhere.*

It's important while combing those racks to discuss what you see with your kids. Their reactions are crucial. It's no failure if a good book is not a mutual hit. Adults and kids are bound to have taste differences. One way to cope with fad influences is to say, "Why don't you get that with your own allowance and I'll buy something we *both* like." It's important to offer your own judgment as balance, not as something forced on them but as an additional boost to their own interest and independence.

I had to learn to contain my own enthusiasm for a while because it threatened my daughter's independence. She would bring home a school mail-order listing of books and ask me which ones I'd choose, then quickly settle on something else. It was a stage she had to go through before we reached the point of mutual respect for each other's tastes, which has led to interesting exchanges of opinion as she learned to articulate her own reactions.

The influence of school peers is enormous and often accounts for a book's overnight success. It will pass from hand to hand like lightning when it achieves "group status." Judy Blume's books flourished by word of mouth long before ad campaigns gave them a boost. Teachers and parents should be quick to spot this as a good starting point and *read what's popular,* whatever it is. The teacher can find out from the kids, and you can find out from the teacher.

The school situation is fertile for exploration, but

it needs parent involvement. Teachers are often so pressed by administrative and curriculum demands that they don't have time for books. It may sound strange to teach reading and literature without books, but that's just what happens. Textbooks and vocabulary lists are substituted for more motivating stories because the results can be easily measured and tested. But many teachers do read out loud and are responsive to parent interest and suggestions.

The school library or media center may be another gold mine or it may need help. Your informed interest will establish a link that leads to a helpful relationship with the person in charge. If there's a good school library, your children should feel at home in it, and your encouragement in the form of a visit can set the precedent as well as turn the school librarian into yet another personal resource for books and information.

PTA involvement often leads to book fairs at school, and there are even brochures available telling how to run one from The Association of American Publishers at 1 Park Avenue, New York, New York 10016.

There are other organizations to turn to outside your locality. The Children's Book Council at 67 Irving Place, New York, New York 10003, has brochures on selecting children's books. The International Reading Association puts out a list of Children's Choices every year which is available from the Children's Book Council. Newspapers and magazines run round-up reviews, especially before Christmas, and bookstores stock up.

If you're interested in dual-language books, it's encouraging to find out that more and more books are being offered in Spanish editions. Children's books are available in every language from French to Japanese.

Ferreting out something new is not the only place to start. Try something old, reliable, rewarding, and easy to find. Attached to this chapter is a list of classics or standard favorites that still live and breathe. Books do have a life of their own. These classics are vital enough to set the reading habit into motion and keep it going toward new horizons.

## CHAPTER 10

### Live Classics*

ALCOTT, LOUISA. *Little Women* (10 & up).
   Meg, Jo, Beth, and Amy are four very different sisters who share good times and bad in this memorable family classic set in the mid-1800s.
BURNETT, FRANCES H. *The Secret Garden* (10 & up).
   A self-centered girl and a pampered invalid boy learn compassion within the walls of an abandoned garden.
CARROLL, LEWIS. *Alice in Wonderland* (10 & up).
   A white rabbit, a mad hatter, and a grinning Cheshire cat—they're all here in this much-loved fantasy about a young girl's extraordinary journey down the rabbit hole.

* These books are all available in many different hardcover and paperback editions.

KIPLING, RUDYARD. *The Jungle Book* (8 & up).
The gripping story of Mowgli, a boy raised in the
jungle by animals that are both wild and wise.

LEAR, EDWARD. *Complete Nonsense Book* (9–12).
Uproarious pictures illustrate this collection of
inspired silliness.

LEWIS, C. S. *The Lion, the Witch, and the Wardrobe*
(10 & up).
A mystical fantasy never lags once the children
step through the magic wardrobe into the land of
Narnia.

MILNE, A. A. *Winnie the Pooh* (6–12).
Christopher Robin, his beloved bear, and a host
of endearing friends romp their way through
happy times in the Hundred-Aker Wood.

STEVENSON, ROBERT LOUIS. *A Child's Garden of Verses*
(6 & up).
Imaginative poems create a rich picture of childhood feelings and dreams.

TWAIN, MARK. *Tom Sawyer* and *Huckleberry Finn* (10
& up).
Exciting books of mystery, dramatic escapades,
and comic misadventures which chronicle the lives
of two boys growing up on the Mississippi River
in the mid-19th century.

WRIGHT, BLANCHE F. *The Real Mother Goose* (4 & up).
More than 150 favorite rhymes, plus many en-
chanting drawings, appear in an edition that has
remained popular for more than 50 years.

ROBERT LAWSON

## *Growing Together*

# 11

I remember walking down a sidewalk with my child and feeling the old familiar tooth-grinding impatience when she stopped to look at a worm. I thought about how late we were and urged her to hurry and finally grabbed her hand and pulled her along with a gentle but determined insistence. She cried. I worried.

I've forgotten what we were late for, but I will never forget that worm. Even looking back, it was an interesting worm. Why didn't I try watching the worm the way she did instead of watching her watch the worm the way I did? I could have learned a lot. I could have seen something of importance about the worm, the child, and myself. Appointments do have to be kept, but worms also have to be watched. And it seems easier for us adults to make appointments than to spare the time to watch worms, though the first may be no more important or interesting or informative than the second.

By the same token, it seems easier to send a kid off to a surefire devouring distraction like Sesame Street or Donald Duck comics. There's nothing wrong with that and we all need to do it sometimes. However, if that's all we do we miss a lot. Every minute and every person counts. Child and adult need each other. Every adult has been a child, and if the child inside the adult dies, something important to adulthood is lost. Children and children's books give voice to the inner child.

I still have some of my childhood books. They are valuable not only because they are old and beautiful, but also because I can never read anything again as a child. They summon a wealth of feelings and associations, and yet I can still appreciate them as an adult.

I feel the same way about my weathered leather mitt and baseball. They were sewn strong and are still good. It's important now to use them both with a child. It can be my child or another child; what's important is to make the connection between the child I was and the child that is. It's a kind of immortality, passing on the book and the baseball mitt. Today's child and tomorrow's child need to add their own new books. That's what keeps us all fresh.

The children's books you want to keep will have a continuity. They will live long and wear well. They will not be the first thing you've grabbed off the checkout stand to silence your squirming grocery-cart rider.

They will be books that you love enough to pass on. For the child, they may represent the heart of family or an escape. I loved it when my parents took turns reading to us all, and I loved turning to the privacy of reading alone.

Any household can be chaotic, from broken toilets to birthday parties. In print there is an ordered world. Books may resemble life, but they have been ordered out of chaos. A children's book is a dream of other things. It is a chance to see through the cracks of life together. The child or adult who wishes for more can find it. Like the important people in life, books that have grown with you stay with you.

## CHAPTER 11

### *Read On*

BADER, BARBARA. *American Picturebooks from Noah's Ark to the Beast Within.* Macmillan.
A lavishly illustrated historical survey shows how the picture book evolved from a medium of entertainment and instruction to a source of artistic enlightenment.

DUFF, ANNIS. *Bequest of Wings: A Family's Pleasure with Books.* Viking.
The joys of sharing books are reflected in this memoir of one family's reading.

EGOFF, SHEILA, et al., eds. *Only Connect: Readings on Children's Literature.* Second edition. Oxford.

Articles written by authors, illustrators, and critics on the many facets of children and their reading.

GILLESPIE, JOHN T., and CHRISTINE B. GILBERT. *Best Books for Children*. Bowker.
Almost 7,000 books for children are briefly described and arranged by subject.

HAZARD, PAUL. *Books, Children and Men*. Horn Book.
An inspiring account of children's literature in several countries.

HUCK, CHARLOTTE. *Children's Literature in Elementary School*. Third revised edition. Holt, Rinehart and Winston.
A textbook that emphasizes child development and the research that reflects the growing importance of literature for a child's language growth and reading achievement.

LAMME, LINDA. *Raising Readers: A Guide to Sharing Literature With Young Children*. Walker.
Practical suggestions for instilling in children an early love of reading.

LARRICK, NANCY. *Encourage Your Child To Read: A Parent's Primer*. Dell Purse Books.
A handy purse book that outlines the basics of reading with your children.

LARRICK, NANCY. *A Parent's Guide to Children's Reading*. Doubleday.
How to help children develop a taste for reading.

LUKENS, REBECCA. *A Critical Handbook of Children's Literature*. Scott, Foresman.
Exploring concepts of theme, plot, style, and tone in children's books.

McCANN, DONNARAE and OLGA RICHARD. *The Child's First Books*. Wilson.

An analysis of children's picture books throughout the history of literature.

SMITH, LILLIAN H. *The Unreluctant Years: A Critical Approach to Children's Literature*. ALA (hardcover); Penguin (paperback).

A look at the literary aspects of children's books.

SUTHERLAND, ZENA. *The Best in Children's Books: The University of Chicago Guide to Children's Literature*. University of Chicago Press.

A collection of reviews from the *Bulletin of the Center for Children's Books* makes an excellent guide to good reading.

TOWNSEND, JOHN ROWE. *A Sounding of Storytellers*. Lippincott.

Insightful essays on British and American children's authors extend this critic's earlier work, *A Sense of Story*.

# Index